The Liturgy
Constitution

The Liturgy Constitution

A Chapter by Chapter Analysis
of the Constitution on the Sacred Liturgy

(With Study-Club Questions)

DEUS BOOKS
PAULIST PRESS
(Paulist Fathers)
Glen Rock, N.J.

NIHIL OBSTAT: Patricius Harris

Censor Deputatus

IMPRIMATUR: ✠ Thomas

Ep. Darensis et Leighlinensis

The Nihil Obstat and Imprimatur are official declarations that a book or pamphlet is free of doctrinal or moral error. No implication is contained therein that those who have granted the Nihil Obstat and Imprimatur agree with the contents, opinions or statements expressed.

COVER DESIGN: Claude Ponsot

Library of Congress
Catalog Card Number: 64-8073

Published by the Paulist Press
Editorial Office: 304 W. 58th St., N.Y., N.Y. 10019
Business Office: Glen Rock, New Jersey 07452

Manufactured in the
United States of America

 24

Contents

6   **Contents**

Promulgation[1]

Pope Paul VI

THE arduous and complex debates have not been without fruit. The discussion of one of the themes, that of the sacred liturgy, has been brought to a satisfactory conclusion. The liturgy was the first subject to be examined and the first too, in a sense, in intrinsic worth and in importance for the life of the Church. We have solemnly promulgated the Constitution on the Sacred Liturgy this day.

This is a source of considerable satisfaction to Us. We note in the Constitution a respect for the hierarchy of values and of duties. God, in the first place; prayer, our first duty; the liturgy, the first source of the divine life which is given to us, the first school of the spiritual life, the first gift which is ours to give to the Christian people who pray with us and share our beliefs; the first invitation to the world to loosen, in true and blessed prayer, its mute tongue, to feel the ineffable regenerative power of chanting with us the praise of God and the hopes of men, through Christ Our Lord and in the Holy Spirit.

[1] An extract from the address by Pope Paul VI at the close of the second session of the Vatican Council, December 4, 1962. The translation is by Father Austin Flannery, O.P.

7

We cannot pass over in silence the careful observance of the liturgy by the faithful of the oriental rites: may they always hold it as a school of truth and may it be for them a flame of love.

It will be well for us to treasure this fruit of our Council: it should animate and characterize the life of the Church. The Church is a religious society, a community of prayer, it is a people among whom the interior life, the life of the spirit, is made to flourish by faith and grace.

If, at this juncture, we have set out to simplify the external expression of worship, in an effort to make it more comprehensible to our people and closer to current speech, this does not mean that we wish to reduce the importance of prayer, or to put it on a lower plane than other obligations of the sacred ministry or of the apostolate. Neither does it mean that we want to make worship less expressive or less esthetically satisfying. It is rather that we want to make it purer, more genuine, closer to the sources of truth and grace, better fitted to be the spiritual patrimony of the people.

To ensure that this will be so, we desire that nobody will meddle with the rules governing the official prayer of the Church, introducing private reforms or special rites; that nobody will claim the right to anticipate arbitrarily the application of the Constitution which We have promulgated today. All must wait until opportune and authoritative instructions will have been issued, and they must await the approval of the reforms which the post-conciliar commissions will prepare.

The nobility of the Church's prayer lies in its harmony throughout the world. Let no man disturb it, let no man meddle with it.

(*L'Osservatore Romano,* December 5, 1963)

A Chapter by Chapter Analysis
of the Liturgy Constitution

The Constitution in the Making[1]

Pierre Marie Gy, O.P.

SOME time after he had announced his intention
of calling an ecumenical council, the late Pope
John XXIII entrusted its preparation to three sec-
retariats and eleven commissions. Of these, the
liturgical commission faced problems which were
posed quite differently from those which most of
the other commissions encountered. These other
commissions—and the Catholic world at large—
began to be aware of problems which up to then
had not been adequately formulated. It was only
after the announcement of the conciliar *aggiorna-
mento* and the inquiry addressed to the bishops
that the Church began actively to consider them,
thus, in many instances, bringing them rapidly to
a head. The problem of the reform of the liturgy,
on the other hand, had already come to a head.
The need for an over-all decision had become im-
perative, a decision by an energetic pope or . . .
by a council.

[1] Reprinted from *La Maison Dieu*, No. 76 (No. 4 of 1963)
by kind permission of the author and the editor. The translation is by Father Austin Flannery, O.P.

THE RENEWAL OF THE LITURGY

A program of liturgical reform had been developing for a number of years. Did it originate with Piux XII's decision to establish a commission for the complete overhauling of the liturgy—a decision re-echoed by *Ephemerides Liturgicae* from 1948—or with the spread of the liturgical apostolate throughout the world? Without doubt it owed its origin to a combination of the two: the visible head of the Church and the whole body, each giving the appropriate response and support to the other. Everything conspired to the same end: there were the echoes awakened by the reforms of Pius XII, even in countries where the liturgical apostolate had scarcely penetrated; the gradual realization by pastors of souls that the liturgical apostolate must needs have repercussions on the very structure of the liturgy; the celebration of the liturgy in missionary contexts, whether in the de-christianized West or the newly evangelized civilizations; the influence of certain great national liturgical centers and the role of the principal members of the Roman commission for reform — Father Ferdinand Antonelli, O.F.M., of the Congregation of Rites, Father (now Cardinal) Augustine Bea, S.J., then private confessor to Pope Pius XII and intermediary between the commission and the Pope, Father G. Löw, prolific author, who died on the eve of the Council; the reception given by the pope of *Mediator Dei* to the representations made to him by the hierarchies of Germany, France and elsewhere, even though it is likely that his personal piety inclined him in a different direction.

Four points, especially, came increasingly to the fore: the pastoral character of the liturgy; its importance for the missions; the necessity of introducing the living languages into the liturgy; the desire for concelebration.

One after another, the different countries came into contact with the liturgical apostolate. Some people, taking their stand on the difficulty of translation, argued that, side by side with the pastoral liturgy, there was a whole section of the liturgy which had no need of being pastoral. Gradually, however, the conviction spread through the Church that the liturgy was wholly and intrinsically pastoral. The Assisi Congress (1956) and the *Instruction* issued in 1958 were, in this respect, decisive steps in the direction of the conciliar constitution. The conviction was gaining ground that it is in its entirety that the liturgy is pastoral.

At the Assisi Congress, especially, it became clear that the liturgical movement had ceased to be confined to a small number of countries and had taken on the dimensions of the Church. This was particularly noticeable in the missionary countries where—thanks to the wide-ranging apostolate of Father Hofinger, the zeal of several bishops and the congresses of Nijmegen and Eichstätt—it began to be accepted that missionary endeavor must needs include the liturgical apostolate.

However, as the liturgical movement spread and as reform succeeded reform, it began to appear that insurmountable obstacles stood in the way of the most important reforms. This was the case with the central question of the language of the liturgy. It is true that bilingual rituals were multiplying and that the privilege of the "German High Mass,"[2]

[2] The "German High Mass" consists of a sung Mass during which the faithful sing vernacular hymns in place of the Creed, etc. It was approved by Rome in 1943 (Translator).

for all that it came under fire several times, was in every instance confirmed and, indeed, was conceded to missionary bishops with little difficulty. But, at the same time, the reading of the epistle and gospel of the Mass by the priest in the vernacular was excluded, or, rather, the decision was left by Pius XII to another pontificate.

It was the same with the question of restoring concelebration. It seems probable that this was seriously considered for Holy Thursday in 1955, it is certain that it was considered in 1957 for the centenary celebrations at Lourdes. However, to make it feasible, it was necessary to settle certain theological controversies and to give a larger dimension to the kind of priestly eucharistic piety which saw concelebration as a pointless and disturbing innovation. Pius XII clearly found the proposal tempting and he set himself to clarify the doctrinal basis for concelebration in his discourse to the members of the Assisi Congress and in a reply by the Holy Office.[3] However, just when concelebration had become a practical possibility, the idea was abandoned.

THE INTERNATIONAL LITURGICAL CONGRESSES

The liturgical reform (and people's understanding of the liturgy) progressed constantly in some sectors and not at all in others, but it received support and inspiration from the international meetings which took place every year from 1950. In 1950, it is true, only France and Germany took part, but from 1951 the meetings were truly inter-

---

[3] Text of Pope Pius' discourse in *The Furrow*, 1956, Oct. and Nov.; *Irish Ecclesiastical Record*, 1956, pp. 344 ff; *Worship*, 1956, Dec., pp. 48 ff. Text of reply of Holy Office in *AAS*, 1957 (39), p. 370. (Translator).

national. Some of them were confined to experts, leading liturgists from the different countries, others were widened to the proportions of congresses. A close liaison was established with the pontifical commission for reform from 1952, and from 1953 its principal members took part successively in the meetings.

One can realize, after the event, the importance of the contacts established between different countries during these years, the usefulness of the collaboration effected and of the work accomplished. Many problems were examined and brought to a head as a result of the discussions which took place at these meetings, from 1950 to 1960, and of the studies undertaken in connection with them. Simultaneously, there developed a widespread desire to see them solved. At the same time, the meetings created a milieu in which many people shared the same pastoral and informed understanding of the liturgy and gained experience of working together.

THE PRE-CONCILIAR COMMISSION

It would seem natural to look to that milieu when staffing the pre-conciliar commission on the liturgy, but it might well be objected that to do so would be to pre-judge the problem of the reform. And, in fact, French and German bishops and the directors of the national liturgical centers, Trier and Paris, were at first excluded. However, it soon became obvious that their help was needed. The following were, in consequence, co-opted onto the commission and played an important part on it: Msgr. H. Jenny, auxiliary bishop of Cambrai, France, Msgr. O. Spuelbeck, apostolic administrator of Meissen, East Germany, Fathers A.-M. Roguet, O.P. and A. G. Martimort, co-directors of the

Center of Pastoral Liturgy, Paris, Msgr. J. Wagner, director of the Liturgical Institute at Trier, Germany.

For the rest, under the authority of its president, Cardinal Gaetano Cicognani, the recruitment of the members of the commission was carried out in obedience to two criteria: that of securing the services of the most effective and competent men, and that of ensuring an equable representation of the different parts of the Church—continents, countries, religious orders. Some people complained that this second criterion was insufficiently observed.

One ought to mention here that Father A. Bugnini, an Italian Lazarist, was a happy choice as secretary. He had been secretary of the commission for reform set up by Pius XII. He was a gifted organizer and possessed an open-minded, pastoral spirit. Many people noted how, with Cardinal Cicognani, he was able to imbue the discussions with the liberty of spirit recommended by Pope John XXIII.

THE PREPARATION OF THE SCHEMA

Father Bugnini has described the work of the commission in an article written for *L'Osservatore Romano* (April 1, 1962). The work was divided among sub-committees, each of them devoting four months of intensive work to one of the thirteen sections of the schema; the liturgical mystery, liturgical formation, active paritcipation, liturgical language, adaptation (chapter one); the Mass, concelebration (chapter two); the sacraments (chapter three); the divine office (chapter four); sacred music (chapter six); sacred art, vestments and furniture (chapter seven); the calendar (appendix). There was a certain amount of repetition, it was found. Thus, the problem of the language of the liturgy cropped up in different sections, and in the end, a special chapter on the liturgical year was added. There was at least one bishop on every sub-committee, but he did not take charge.

The texts composed by the sub-committees took their places in the complete schema, which was examined in its entirety three times: in the session held in April 1961, again by means of a written consultation and, finally, in the session held in January 1962.

The commission had to prepare a conciliar document, an undertaking of which none of its members had had previous experience. It was a task for which—and all the pre-conciliar commissions had a similar experience—liturgical or theological competence do not suffice, nor is any specialized knowledge of much avail. What is needed is a minimum of knowledge of the great Councils, a broad outlook and a certain intuitive awareness of the signs of the times.

There were two preliminary problems, on whose solution most of the rest of the work would depend. Should the document confine itself to the Latin liturgy? Should it be practical, containing only decisions on reform, or should these be afforded a theological justification?

The first question was indeed a very important one: the Council was not to be a Council of the Latin Church, but an Ecumenical Council. Was it right that the preparatory commission should confine itself to the Latin liturgy? Further, one has not properly posed the problem of the language of the Latin liturgy unless one has situated the Latin Church in the totality of the *Catholica*. On the other hand, in most of the Oriental Churches, the problem of reform, urgent as it might be, cannot be examined seriously save in the context of dialogue between the Churches which are in communion with Rome and those which are not. It was necessary, therefore, to leave this question aside, to treat only of the reform of the Roman liturgy, referring, as need arose, to examples from the Oriental Churches (in the case of concelebration, for example), eventually enunciating principles whose validity would not be limited to the Western liturgy.

The solution of the second problem was obvious at once: the document ought to be at once disciplinary and doctrinal. In conciliar categories, it ought to be, not a simple decree, but a constitution. In this connection one can only regret that the preconciliar ruling on mixed commissions did not operate so as to permit collaboration with the theological commission.

Once it had been decided to prepare a schema which would be at once doctrinal and practical, the next thing was to discover, gradually, the style that was appropriate to it. According to the tradition of the Council of Trent and even of Vatican I, it should be biblical and patristic, and should maintain a certain distance from theological disputes. But should one not, at the same time, take account of the doctrinal style of the encyclicals, which are more concerned with theological precisions and are somewhat removed from biblical theology? The question was all the more relevant since Pius XII had devoted considerable attention to the liturgy, in the encyclical, *Mediator Dei,* and elsewhere. Should the conciliar constitution be a solemn prolongation of the Pope's teaching? Could it conceivably abstract from it?

Little by little a delicate solution emerged, a solution which seems to have pleased the Council Fathers and to have inspired even the theological commission in its revision of schemas. The style of the Constitution, it was decided, would be that traditionally adopted in Councils; it would be wholly biblical, except where canonical precision was necessary. Thus it is that the opening pages, on the history of salvation, are closer to biblical theology than to the style of *Mediator Dei*. However, at the same time, the Constitution relies considerably on the great encyclical of Pius XII and time and again it uses its very terminology, without quotation marks or reference. Only in the case of biblical, liturgical and patristic quotations are references given.

One problem that arose was whether or not the schema should enter into details. In certain cases it was obviously desirable to have a program of reform precise enough to be sure of implementation. If the formulation of the Council's proposal was too vague, one would risk giving the conciliar fathers the impression that they were being asked to issue *carte blanche* in the matter of liturgical reform. On the other hand, a detailed program of reform was not worthy of an ecumenical council nor in keeping with its role. The result, in fact, was a schema which outlined the principles of reform, what John XXIII called, *apropos* of the breviary, "the higher principles, *altiora principia*," the schema itself, however, being accompanied by *Declarationes,* an explanatory commentary destined for the conciliar Fathers. During the conciliar debates of October and November 1962, there were several complaints that the *Declarationes* had not been distributed. At length this omission was remedied in part. *The Declarationes* are the base of the schema, it is they which give it its density. They are like the lower part of an iceberg, the most important part, for all that it remains hidden under the water. However, the *Declarationes* are not in any sense binding on the post-conciliar commission.

THE SCHEMA IS PRESENTED IN THE COUNCIL

The schema prepared by the liturgical commission was given its definitive shape and was accepted by a plenary session in a vote taken on January 23, 1962. Duplicated copies were at once made, for transmission to the central commission. The program of reform was so vast that it caused the president, Cardinal Gaetano Cicognani, to hesitate; he waited a week and signed the document on February 1. He died on February 5.

Cardinal Cicognani's successor was appointed on February 22; he was Cardinal Larraona. That same day the Holy Father promulgated the Constitution, *Veterum Sapientia,* which, among other prescriptions, forbade any attack on the use of Latin in the liturgy. Subsequently, the schema was discussed by the central commission, in which the balance of tendencies was very different from what it was to be in the Council. The schema was later subjected to restrictive changes. Father Bugnini, who had shared the helm with the late Cardinal Cicognani, lost his chair at the Lateran and was not made secretary of the conciliar commission subsequently.

The Council began on October 11, 1962 and the Fathers set about electing the members of the conciliar commissions. Six of the bishops elected to the liturgical commission had belonged to the preconciliar liturgical commission. Among others, one must single out Cardinal Giacomo Lercaro, who for years had been one of the leaders of the liturgical movement, and Msgr. G. Van Bekkum, the spokesman for the liturgy of the missions. The secretary of the commission was Father Ferdinand Antonelli, O.F.M., who had figured prominently on the commission for reform set up by Pius XII.

THE DEBATE ON THE SCHEMA

The debate on the schema occupied fifteen general congregations (October 22 to November 13). The debate was badly organized, but it was extremely useful, even when it was long-drawn and repetitious.[4] It gave a chance to the Fathers who were not fully abreast of developments to inform themselves and make up their minds on the general problems put by the schema (doctrinal style of the Council, role of the bishops' conferences) and on the reform of the liturgy itself. The Council not merely revealed a common denominator preexistant among the bishops, it quickly enough created a new one. Public debate revealed the true worth of authorities and arguments. Above all, in spite of the diversity of situations within the Church, there was agreement on the necessity of reform. The young Churches and Latin America went further in their demands for vernacular liturgy and adaptation than did the pre-conciliar commission. Once again, the question of liturgical language was central to these debates. It is likely that there is no argument, pro or con, of any weight or worth, which was not heard in St. Peter's during those days.

---

[4] There were 328 oral interventions (Cardinal Ruffini, 6 times; Cardinals Léger and Spellman, 4 times each) and more than 350 written interventions.

Among the questions which were most in the forefront of the debate, that of communion under both kinds met particular opposition. One wonders if that part of the Constitution would have been passed if it had been put to a separate vote.

On the question of the reform of the divine office, the majority—which was apparent enough after the debate had commenced—was divided between a multitude of contradictory opinions. One had here, as was evident during the preparation of the schema, a question almost as difficult as that of the language of the liturgy. The reason for this was a certain tension inherent in Christian prayer, especially in the prayer of the apostle, and caused by the absence of the absolute criteria afforded by the divine institution in other parts of the liturgy.[5] It may also be caused by the illusions or the hypocrisy which have often accumulated in this domain.

Lastly, it is to be noted that while sacred music is of considerable importance—and, indeed, some people wanted to give it a central place in the schema —it attracted little attention in the Council.

APPROVAL AND AMENDMENTS

On November 14, the Council gave massive approval, in principle, to the schema on the liturgy (2162 *placet,* 46 *non placet*). It remained for the conciliar commission—which set to work slowly at first, picking up speed as it went on—to analyze the written text of all the interventions by the Fathers, extracting from them the amendments the Council desired. This enormous task was com-

---

[5] Thus, since Christ instituted the sacraments and, in several of them, gave very precise directives, we are in possession of absolute standards of judgment in that domain; not so, however, with regard to the divine office.— (Translator).

pleted, with regard to the Introduction and the first chapter (one-third of the Constitution), in about a month. The amendments to Articles 1 to 46 were voted on between November 17 and December 6, 1962. The revision of the Constitution was completed between the two sessions and the remaining amendments were voted on during the second session.

Each chapter was submitted to a final vote, the terms being: *placet, placet juxta modum,* or *non placet,* the *placet juxta modum* being counted with the *placets.* It was the task of the commission, however, to take back to the Council Fathers the results of its deliberations on the *modi*—the desired amendments. It was the opinion of all that it did this with extreme fidelity. In two cases, especially for the Mass (781 votes *juxta modum*) and for the sacraments (1,054 votes *juxta modum*), the commission thought it best to present new amendments, which gave to the ordinary of the place (*ordinarius loci*) a general control over concelebration in his diocese, and submitting, without restriction, the choice of the language of the sacraments to episcopal conferences. The voting took place on November 22.

If one considers the amendments to the Constitution as a whole, including those added while the *Modi* (*i.e.* changes suggested by Fathers who voted *placet juxta modum*) were being examined, a large number of them will be seen to concern particular points which were either reinforced or softened, or were clarified and made more precise. Two classes of amendment, however, are worthy of mention. One class concerns doctrine and, ultimately, doctrinal continuity between Vatican II and Trent;

the other class concerns the use of the vernacular at present and for the future.

If, from the point of view of ecclesiology, Vatican II corresponds, in a sense, with Vatican I and complements it, from the point of view of the theology of the liturgy and of the sacraments—and of the whole attitude to liturgical reform—it is with Trent that comparison seems relevant. At the present time, certainly, there is no need for the Catholic Church to remain on the defensive, to be content to affirm what the reformers questioned. The Church owes it to the faithful—and, ultimately, to Our Lord—to resume all that is evangelically valid in the liturgical perceptions of the reformers. The observers at the Council have rightly emphasized this aspect of the Council's achievement. On the other hand, however, the Church must assert her teaching's accord with earlier Councils, and the complete homogeneity of the faith. A number of amendments inserted at the behest of the Fathers— several of them referring to the sacrificial character of the eucharist—served to underline this last point.

During the debates and the voting on the language of the liturgy, the Council, with its pastoral bias, showed that there was no justification for the vicissitudes suffered by the schema in the spring and summer of 1962. In the council chamber, it won the assent of an assembly, some of whose members favored more conservative, and others more advanced, measures than those outlined in the text of the schema. It was obvious, however, that an Ecumenical Council must do more than meet the needs of the present; it must also foresee future developments and must shape them. It must make provision for an increasing use of the vernacular, for new adaptations and, even, for the emergence of new liturgical rites over and above those now in use in East and West. Too radical a change would be a pastoral evil. At the same time, the Council must guide, pastorally, today's and tomorrow's progressive evolution.

Pope Paul VI, who presided over the second session of the Council, was one of those who, on October 22, 1962, on the first day of the debate, gave the schema his support. When, as head of the Church, he promulgated the Constitution on December 4, 1964, he underlined the importance of the liturgy: "the first to be examined and the first, too, in a sense, by reason of its intrinsic value and its importance in the life of the Church."

Discussion Questions

1. A program of liturgical reform had been developing for a number of years. Explain.
2. What four points on the liturgy, especially, came increasingly to the fore prior to the Second Vatican Council?
3. What is the "German High Mass?"
4. Do you think concelebration is a pointless and disturbing innovation?
5. Mention some of the members of the pre-conciliar commission on the liturgy.
6. What were the thirteen sections of the schema?
7. What were the two preliminary problems, on whose solution most of the rest of the work would depend?
8. What elements determined the style of the Constitution?
9. What question met with particular opposition?
10. What question attracted little attention in the Council?
11. Why does the Church owe it to the faithful to resume all that is evangelically valid in the liturgical perceptions of the reformers?
12. When Paul VI promulgated the Constitution on December 4, 1964, how did he underline the importance of the liturgy?

My Apostolate

1. The liturgy was the first subject to be examined by the Second Vatican Council and the first too, in a sense, in intrinsic worth and in importance for the life of the Church. It was an attempt to make the Church's worship purer, more genuine, closer to the sources of truth and grace and better fitted to the spiritual patrimony of the faithful. To insure its success, I shall do my best to study the *Constitution on the Sacred Liturgy* and to grasp the clear and penetrating directives laid down by the Council.

1 General Principles

Colman O'Neill, O.P.

IN conformity with the stated aims of the Council, the *Constitution on the Sacred Liturgy* is primarily a pastoral document. It is concerned, that is to say, with the broad principles which are to govern the adaptation of the liturgy so that it may become again what it once was, and what it is meant to be: a form of worship and sanctification which genuinely corresponds to the needs of Christians. This first published result of the Council's discussions may be fairly assessed and accurately interpreted only in these practical perspectives.

That some form of adaptation of the liturgy was called for has been clear for some time to those whose duty in the Church brings them into immediate contact with large groups of the faithful. The Council has shown itself to be thoroughly aware of the difficulties of the parish priest who wants to see his people taking part with appreciation and profit in the Mass and the celebration of the sacraments. And it has gotten to the heart of the matter in a quite remarkable way. With a deft and sure hand it has laid bare the central reality of the liturgy, separating what is essential from what is the product of two thousand years of history, and has gone on to formulate practical norms, derived

27

from what is central and essential and orientated by pastoral experience.

Pastors and laity who have grasped the meaning and importance of the liturgy can only rejoice at the clear and penetrating directives laid down by the Council. The same may be said for theologians; for the theologian too is concerned with the practical consequences of his science; and in this Constitution he can find concrete expression, in the form of laws governing the practice of every Catholic church in the world, given to some of the most profound truths of the Christian faith. It is not always that the contemplative can see the ideas to which he is committed being realized in action. Could this happen, at least on such a scale, anywhere but in the Church of Christ?

In order to achieve what may, without exaggeration, be called a masterpiece of legislation, the Council had to refer to the nature of the liturgy as it has been revealed; for the Church is never, and cannot be, merely pragmatic. In harmony with their aim, the conciliar Fathers have sought out and proclaimed with almost painful, certainly dramatic, single-mindedness, the inner reality of the liturgy. God, working through Christ, active in the Church, saving mankind, is there. His activity takes shape in the Church in word and ritual. Men must discover him there and open themselves to him. And to do this they must understand the word and ritual and be able to adopt them as the natural expression of their own desire for God.

This approach seeks the significance of the liturgy by adopting the method which the First Vatican Council described as discovering the connection which exists between the various revealed mysteries. It is one of the processes of theology. The theologian must prepare for it, and complement it, with analysis of each detail of the mysteries. And here a note of warning must be sounded. Because analysis is so essential a part of his science there is the possibility that the professional theologian will be disappointed with the *Constitution on the Sacred Liturgy;* for only vestigial traces of the analytic process appear there. To entertain such disappointment would be to misunderstand the purpose of the present Council. Lack of emphasis on the analytic element of theology certainly characterizes the reported discussions of conciliar problems. But, it must be remembered, the conciliar Fathers deliberately chose a mode of procedure adapted to Christianity in the mid-twentieth century. The present circumstances of the Church require a return to essentials, to sources, to the breathtaking simplicity of the complex design of God for bringing his people to himself. Because it follows this line the *Constitution on the Sacred Liturgy* presents a more dramatic form of teaching than that proposed by Pius XII in his encyclical letter, *Mediator Dei;* but this encyclical will nevertheless remain the basic authoritative analysis of the liturgy. On several points the encyclical is more explicit and more developed theologically than the Council. In particular there springs to mind Pius XII's noteworthy teaching on the baptismal character and on the participation of the faithful in the Mass.

The success of the *Constitution on the Sacred Liturgy* is assured. Principally a pastoral Council, Vatican II has produced an enlightened revision of legislation that is unparalleled in Church history. It was guided by a vision of the essentials of the liturgical mystery. The way it formulates these essentials is striking and forceful.

INTRODUCTION

Three brief articles which serve as Introduction to the Constitution indicate the importance, within the context of the Council's aims, of discussing the liturgy. The second article is noteworthy for the concise and profound description it gives of the Church.

Art. 2. Anticipating what is to be explained more fully in chapter one, the article states that in the liturgy, particularly in the Mass, "the work of our redemption is carried forward,"[1] and for this reason its celebration serves to express and to display to others both the mystery of Christ and the authentic nature of the true Church. That it gives expression to the mystery of Christ is clear, for the liturgy *is* part of the mystery of Christian redemption being realized in the world today. For this very reason the liturgy also manifests the true nature of the Church, since the Church is nothing else than the place in which the mystery of redemption is being realized. The liturgy is the most characteristic and the most efficacious activity of the Church; and the qualities which are to be found in the liturgy are the qualities which belong to the Church. To both may be applied, consequently, the description which is given to the latter:

[1] The text used in the preparation of this commentary was the Latin original, published with a German translation commissioned by the German, Austrian, and Swiss bishops (Rome 1963). Subsequently, English translations have been largely brought into conformity with the translation prepared by Father C. Howell, S.J. (Cirencester 1963).

It is of the essence of the Church that she be both human and divine, visible and yet endowed with invisible realities, eager to act and yet intent on contemplation, present in this world and yet not at home in it; and she is all these things in such wise that in her the human is directed and subordinated to the divine, the visible likewise to the invisible, action to contemplation, and this present world to that city yet to come, which we seek.

Not only, then, does the liturgy build up the mystical body of those who already belong to Christ; it also serves, as a natural consequence of this, to bring the Church before the eyes of the world as the living mystery of Christian salvation.

CHAPTER ONE

GENERAL PRINCIPLES

The chapter, as its title indicates, deals with the general principles which are to govern the restoration, or adaptation, and the promotion of the liturgy. The text of the Constitution itself is divided into four principal sections; but, in harmony with the themes discussed, the chapter may be divided, for the sake of simplicity, into the following two parts with their sub-divisions:

I (a) The nature of the liturgy.

   (b) Its importance in the life of the Church.

II Promotion of the faithful's participation.

   (a) The faithful's participation.

   (b) Instruction of the clergy.

   (c) Adaptation of the text and ritual.

   (d) Liturgical significance of the diocese and parish.

(e) Promotion of the pastoral-liturgical movement.

I (a) THE NATURE OF THE LITURGY (Arts. 5-8).

Art. 5. Salvation is seen under its fundamental aspect as a divine initiative which takes definitive
form in the mission of the Word in the Incarnation. This mission was foreshadowed in God's care
for his people in the Old Testament and its potentialities are fulfilled in the Church.

The humanity of Christ, united to the divine
Word, was accordingly the instrument of our salvation, so that in Christ "the perfect achievement
of our reconciliation came forth, and the fullness
of divine worship was given to us." The twofold
significance which is here indicated in Christ's
earthly mission is to be discovered principally in
his passion, resurrection and ascension. These three
events form the single paschal mystery, so called
because it was the fulfillment by Christ, in the history of mankind's salvation, of the Exodus of the
Israelites from captivity and of the Jewish paschal
liturgy which commemorated that divine saving
action.

In this supreme mystery Christ "dying, destroyed
our death and rising, restored our life." The
traditional image of the Church issuing from the
side of the crucified Christ expresses the truth that
Christ's death and resurrection are effective for us
only through the ministrations of the Church. For
this reason the Church is called a "sacrament" or
a "mystery" (both words translate *sacramentum*);
for it is the visible presence in the world of the
ever-active central mystery of Christ's Pasch; and,
through the visible actions of the Church, Christ's
Pasch effectively saves individual men.

Art. 6. The metaphorical description of the Church as issuing from the side of the dying Christ is now reduced to more literal and more explicit terms; in this process the place of the liturgy in the Church is more clearly defined.

Being sent by Christ and being filled with the Holy Spirit, the apostles shared in the mission from the Father of the Word made flesh. Their function in the Church was firstly one of preaching the Gospel of salvation through Christ; but, in addition to this, they were to "exercise, by means of sacrifice and sacraments, the work of salvation which they had proclaimed." This is a particularly felicitous account of the mission of the apostles and of their successors. It distinguishes the two functions of preaching and administering the sacramental system; and at the same time it indicates how the second is a development of the first. These two, word and sacrament, are indissolubly linked in the Church. The liturgy is a form of preaching Christ to which a new dimension of reality has been given by God. Because of their sacramental power the apostles not merely presented a verbal account of the mystery of Christ, an account which, for all the undoubted power of the Spirit accompanying it and working through it, remained an objective appeal to the mind and heart of those who heard it; they could too, in the Mass and the sacraments, actually bring the faithful into mysterious and efficacious contact with the paschal mystery of Christ itself.

So in baptism men are "inserted" sacramentally into Christ's mystery. The sacrament unites them to Christ in such a way that his death, burial and resurrection are theirs. Being constituted members of Christ by baptism, they are thereby drawn into that mystical union with him which, according to the divine design, associates them with his supreme work of satisfaction and merit. This association affects them personally so that they undergo an inward, moral rebirth. The life of sin which was theirs is put off; and in this sense they die and are buried. The new life of grace is given them through Christ; and in this sense they rise from the grave, re-born as adopted sons of the Father, qualified to join themselves with Christ in his true adoration of the Father (*cf.* John 4, 23). Similarly, as St. Paul teaches (1 Cor. 11, 26), when they take part in "the Lord's supper," they are associated mysteriously with the unique sacrifice of Christ and draw upon its saving efficacy; and this the faithful will continue to do until a new form of union with Christ is made possible in his Second Coming.

Article Six concludes with an account of how, according to the New Testament, the Church carried out the twofold function entrusted to the apostles.

Art. 7. From what has been said it begins to emerge that there is a legitimate sense in which the Church may be said to "complete" or "perfect" the work of salvation. Very far from detracting from Christ's unique role as Mediator of salvation, the mediatory function of the Church, since it derives from his, and is subordinated to his, is the supreme proof of the efficacy of his mediation. For the Church never acts independently of Christ; he is always present and active in her saving actions, giving them their power. The mode of his presence varies according to the nature of the Church's action. There is the supreme form of his presence in the eucharist; but he is present also in the person of the celebrant at Mass in such fashion that it is Christ himself who offers through the priest's ministry. He is present in the other sacraments in a less perfect, but no less true, manner; for it is by his power that the sacraments produce their saving effects. In its formulation of this teaching the Council deliberately retains the traditional expressions which are sufficiently broad to permit of varying theological interpretations. Further, and clearly different, forms of the presence of Christ are realized through the Scriptures when they are read in Church ritual, and, finally, in the prayer of the Church. Christ speaks through the Scriptures; he worships with the Church.

In the second paragraph of this article an important principle is introduced. When he is present in her actions Christ always associates the Church with him in the two aspects of his saving activity, namely, the worship of God and the sanctification of men. In this association is preserved the twofold relation of the Church to Christ. On the one hand she is wholly dependent on his redemption for all her good works and "calls upon him as her Lord"; on the other hand, and as a consequence of the first, she herself worships the Father through him, co-operating with him as his Spouse.[2]

The teaching of the first articles is summed up in a definition of the liturgy as "the exercise of the priestly office of Christ in which the sanctification of man is signified by signs perceptible to the

---

[2] The relation of the faithful to Christ in worship is more fully developed in *Mediator Dei cf.* CTS [Eng.] ed. §§ 96-98), where, in reference to the Mass, an important distinction is made between offering "through" and "with." *Cf. Constit.,* ch. 2, art. 48.

senses, and is effected in a way which corresponds with each of these signs, and in which also full public worship is performed by the mystical body of Jesus Christ, that is, by the head and his members." Such a definition justifies the immediate conclusion that celebration of the liturgy is the supreme form of sacred action, unequaled in efficacy by any other action of the Church. For no other action can lay claim to derive its value from so close a relation to the action of Christ or to procure such rich fruits. (This is the sense of the words: "by the same title and to the same degree.")

Art. 8. Before concluding the exposition of the nature of the liturgy, the Constitution draws attention to its eschatological significance. Whoever takes part in the earthly liturgy thereby shares in anticipatory fashion in the worship of heaven. The theology developed particularly in the Epistle to the Hebrews is recognizable in this view of the liturgy. Because Christ, the risen Head, has already penetrated in his humanity into the heavenly sanctuary, those of his members who join with him in worship of the Father are drawn into participation in the liturgy of the angels and saints. It is the hope of the earthly members that they will join the company of the saints when Christ comes to bestow the full fruits of salvation in glory.

(b) THE IMPORTANCE OF THE LITURGY IN THE LIFE OF THE CHURCH (Arts. 9-13)

The importance of the liturgy is already apparent from the account of its nature; but in these five articles the Constitution further outlines the liturgy's relationship with other actions of the Church.

Art 9. The limitations of the liturgy are first defined. In spite of its perfection it does not constitute the entire activity of the Church; and indeed men cannot participate in the liturgy unless preachers have first proclaimed to them the Word of God; and, in their turn, preachers depend for their authority on the mission they have received from those who hold jurisdiction in the Church. Not only, then, must the Church call unbelievers to faith in Christ and to repentance; she must continue to preach the same message to believers so that they may be disposed to receive the sacraments profitably. She must teach them to observe the commandments and encourage them to perform "works of charity and piety" and to exercise the apostolate. (The word translated as "piety" is *pietas,* which has a technical sense in theology. The Constitution appears to use it in the non-technical sense expressed by the English word.)

Art. 10. Nevertheless, the liturgy remains the central activity of the Church; for it is both the summit toward which every other action is directed and the source from which the Church draws her strength. Each aspect is in turn developed in this article. The text calls for no comment, apart from the description of the eucharist as the "renewal of the alliance between God and men." The redemptive act of Calvary is here considered as the consummation of the Old Alliance between God and Israel and as the seal placed on the New Alliance. For in the person of the Word Incarnate, as he offered his sacrifice, were united both the saving initiative of God and the consequent loving response of man. Here is the supreme expression of the New Alliance and it is only by participation in it that men can be saved. Their participation is achieved by their union with the response of Christ in his humanity to his Father; and this means

union with Christ in charity. When Mass is offered
and Communion received men enter anew into the
Alliance of Christ; the effect of this must be that
those who have taken part worthily in the celebration will be urged to the exercise of charity.

Art. 11. It is in this context, where both the
limitations and the supremacy of the liturgy are
stressed, that the question of the participation of
the faithful is first introduced. The present article
recalls what is required if the liturgy is to achieve
its full efficacy. On the part of the faithful are
necessary good dispositions, sincerity in performing
whatever part of the ritual may be assigned them,
and cooperation with grace. On the part of pastors
this implies care that the faithful should participate "consciously, actively and fruitfully." No
definition is given here of the term "actively,"
actuose.[3]

Art. 12. Liturgical participation, however, does
not exhaust the demands of the Christian life.
Private prayer and mortification are also necessary;
and indeed these are the indispensable prerequi-
sites and consequences of true liturgical participation.

Art. 13. It follows clearly that approved forms
of prayer which are not liturgical are worthy of
high commendation. That they should be in harmony with the liturgy and should lead the faithful
toward it is apparent from what has been said of
the central place held by the liturgy.

---

[3] Father C. Howell, S.J., loc. cit., has: "fully aware of what
they are doing, actively engaged in the rite, and enriched
by its effects"; but this is a commentary—however justified
—rather than a translation. The German translation is
more circumspect with: "bewusst, tätig und mit geistlichem
Gewinn."

II PROMOTION OF THE FAITHFUL'S PARTICIPATION

(a) THE FAITHFUL'S PARTICIPATION (Art. 14)

By way of introduction to regulations concerning the instruction of the clergy, the Constitution makes certain observations on the participation of the faithful. Since it is in view of promoting such participation that all the subsequent rules are formulated, what is said in various articles about participation itself may usefully be considered first.

Already in Art. 7 it has been noted that Christ always associates the Church with his worship of the Father and his santification of men. This applies, though in diverse ways, to both clergy and faithful. Art. 14 expresses the urgent desire of the Church, in her function as Mother, that "all the faithful be led to that full, conscious and active participation in liturgical celebrations which is demanded by the very nature of the liturgy itself" and in respect of which the Christian people, the royal priesthood (*cf.* 1 Pet. 2, 9; 2, 4-5), has both right and duty by reason of baptism. The same article goes on to state that "this full and active participation by all the people is the primary and indispensable source from which the faithful are to derive the true Christian spirit." But what is the precise nature of this participation? Or rather, in order to keep the problem at the practical level which the Constitution favors, what exact form should this participation take?

There can be no doubt that the Council considers it desirable that the faithful should take part in the Mass, for example, by the fullest possible participation in the ritual, answering the responses and joining in the singing, and so on. Does Art. 14

mean that only in this way is the nature of the liturgy fulfilled, and that this form of participation is the primary and *indispensable* source of the true Christian spirit? It must be confessed that no explicit answer is given in the text to this urgent problem. An indication of certain reservations to be made is contained in Art. 19 which distinguishes between internal and external active participation and which admits that the fullest mode of active participation is not in every circumstance feasible. Pastors, it is there stated, must make allowance for differences of age, condition (presumably, sickness and health), way of life (whether, for example, a member of a religious congregation or not) and standard of religious culture. It is necessary on general theological grounds to hold that the conciliar Fathers did not intend to place limits to the internal participation (acts of religion, charity) of any person. It is without doubt at the level of external participation in the ritual that the necessity of allowing for greater or less activity is acknowledged.

From this it is clear that the *indispensable* source of the true Christian spirit is not full external participation. It is, in other words, possible to take part in the liturgy authentically without answering all the responses or singing all that could be sung. From this it follows that the nature of the liturgy does not require full external participation as an inseparable property. It appears necessary to make these distinctions lest imprudent use should be made of Art. 14 as though it required full external participation as an absolute condition for any form of participation whatsoever. Such a maximalist interpretation being excluded, it must be readily acknowledged that the mind of the Council very clearly is that every effort should be made to introduce the faithful to the fullest possible external participation. Only when this is procured will the natural sense of the liturgical symbolism have been satisfied.

By way of theological commentary the following may be said. Participation in the liturgy cannot be exclusively internal. The very nature of the action demands that participation be also external. But simple—so-called "passive"—attendance at Mass or simple reception of the sacraments are already in themselves external participation. Without doubt the pastoral aim of the Church is that such minimal external participation (which derives from possession of the baptismal character) should be developed to the fullest degree possible. The full potentialities of the liturgy as an action of common worship could be realized only if all the faithful participated fully in the ritual; and each of the faithful should make this his aim. But, as Art. 19 indicates, such an ideal is hardly compatible with the vastly differentiated character of the individuals who make up "the faithful." It will be for local bishops to decide, taking account of the Council's wishes, in what measure external participation will be helpful to the majority of their people.

(b) INSTRUCTION OF THE CLERGY (Arts. 15-18)

The prescriptions are of a practical nature. The terms used in Art. 16—curiously enough in the context—have been given a popular, rather than a theological, signification. It should not be thought, for example, that the enumeration of aspects of the liturgy—theological, historical, spiritual, pastoral, juridical—implies that the last four are non-theological. The exact sense of "theological" here is

probably "dogmatic" or "systematic." Nor is it
suggested that the object of theology is "the mystery of Christ and the history of salvation." It is a
question simply of the practical orientation of
theology lectures.

(c) ADAPTATION OF THE TEXT AND RITUAL
(Arts. 21-40)

Art. 21 clearly defines the limits set to adaptation of the liturgy. It concerns only the text and
the ritual; and the rule guiding it is the faithful's
power of understanding. The necessary qualifica-
tion is added: "insofar as possible"; for the liturgy
is in the final analysis a mystery.

Among the general directive norms, noteworthy
is the stress laid in Art. 24 on the place of Scripture
in the liturgy. The Scriptures are not simply the
material source from which the text of the liturgy
is drawn, either directly or indirectly. The liturgy,
because it is the activation of the mystery of Christ,
is a sacramental celebration of the Scriptures. The
word of the liturgy is the word of the Scriptures;
and in the liturgy the Scriptures acquire new saving effectiveness because Christ is present and active
in a special way in these Church actions. Art. 35
returns to this theme, showing how the homily also,
if based on the Scriptures and the liturgy, becomes
"a proclamation of God's wonderful works in the
history of salvation or in the mystery of Christ ever
made present and active within us, especially in the
celebration of the liturgy."

Arts. 26-32 formulate rules for adaptation based
on the fact that the liturgy is an action of the
whole Church, involving not only ordained ministers but also the body of the faithful. As Art. 26
stresses, though certain functions in the liturgy are

reserved to those in sacred orders, the integral action of the liturgy belongs to the whole Church and shares in the nature of the Church. And the Church, in spite of its being divided into rulers and those ruled, is a unified body, with the parts cooperating harmoniously in view of attaining a single purpose. The Church, both in its structure and in its worship, is a "sacrament" or visible manifestation of unity; and in liturgical action this unity is further deepened by Christ.

In the very nature of things, the liturgy, no matter how it is externally celebrated, activates in this way the unity of the Church. This is particularly true of the Mass; and it would be a dangerous aberration if the Council's desire for full external participation were to be interpreted as some kind of condemnation of what are popularly known as "private" Masses. It is a fact that in certain continental religious communities the practice has been introduced of priests attending the conventual Mass and receiving Communion during it, instead of celebrating personally. While respect is owed the individual's conscience, it must be maintained that if such a practice were to become general the nature of the Mass would be gravely misunderstood. This is something, it seems safe to assert, which the ordinary Catholic's common sense makes clear to him; it can also be demonstrated theologically. It is to be hoped that the brief reference to the matter in Art. 27—"every Mass has of itself a public and social nature"—will not be overlooked.

The rules deriving from the didactic and pastoral character of the liturgy (Arts. 33-36) serve to emphasize once again that the liturgy is a celebration of the Word of God in which God speaks through Christ and the people respond to his invitation. The prayers of the community and the symbolic actions performed are all meant to speak to the minds and hearts of the participants, and to encourage them to render intelligent and willing service to God. Such a purpose obviously cannot be achieved if the people do not understand what is going on; whence the need for simplicity and brevity in the ritual (Arts. 33-34). It is in this context that the agitated question of Latin is considered; prudently, no universal solution is proposed, a limited faculty of introducing the vernacular being extended to local authorities (Art. 36).

Similar principles are applied to adaptation of liturgical ceremonial to local and racial customs; and a similar limited faculty of modification is granted (Arts. 37-40).

(d) LITURGICAL SIGNIFICATION OF DIOCESE AND PARISH (Arts. 41-42)

The genius of the Constitution for getting to the heart of things and sketching out in broad strokes the essentials of the liturgy is again exemplified in this section. The liturgy, as the people see it celebrated, is scattered, as it were, piecemeal throughout all the churches and chapels of the world. All the local celebrations are certainly united invisibly by reason of the union of each priest and each member of the faithful with Christ. But with the liturgy, as with the Church, what is invisible is always accompanied by and expressed by a visible element. So it is with unity. The bishop is its visible center in each diocese. Christ is the unique High Priest; the bishop is for his own flock Christ's representative and is, therefore, the visible high priest of his diocese. Though he is not always able

to exercise his pastoral office directly in respect of
all his flock, he retains, ideally at least, a control-
ling influence on the liturgical life of the diocese.
It is he, normally, who ordains and confirms; and
and it is he who consecrates the materials used in
several of the sacraments.

The liturgical unity of the diocese would be
ideally signified if all the priests and all the faithful
were grouped around the bishop in a single celebration (Art. 41). Evidently, it is only in the rarest
circumstances that such symbolism can be created.
Practical requirements dictate that the smaller
groupings of parishes be set up within each diocese;
and then the symbol of liturgical unity is best
achieved when the local parishioners are grouped
around their parish priest. Common parish worship
is calculated to encourage the growth of that com-
munity-awareness which should be characteristic
of those who form one body in Christ, united in
charity.

The Constitution passes over in silence the
obvious difficulty that the order of priests is not
organized exclusively on a diocesan basis. This
means that the Mass, the principal act of the liturgy, and of the Church, is not necessarily a diocesan or parochial act. It is quite true that the greater
part of the faithful belongs to one or other diocese
and parish and, for this reason, the parish Mass
has a particular significance. The Constitution
justly lays stress on the importance of Sunday Mass
in this respect; but even here it hardly appears that
the present juridico-sacramental constitution of the
Church, with its provision for religious orders and
congregations, necessarily requires attendance at
the parish church. In harmony with the spirit of
the Constitution, the existence of religious orders

should be seen, not as a threat to the unity of the Church, but as a witness to the rich diversity of Catholicism. Wherever Mass is celebrated the Church is one in Christ.

(e) PROMOTION OF THE PASTORAL-LITURGICAL MOVEMENT (Arts. 43-46)

Introducing regulations concerning the establishment of various commissions, the Constitution significantly describes the liturgical movement as a sign of the providential dispositions of God for the present age and as the passing of the Spirit through his Church. The provisions made by the Council are themselves among the principal manifestations of this divine intervention.

Discussion Questions

1. Why is it that the Church is never, and cannot be, merely pragmatic?
2. Is the Constitution primarily a pastoral document?
3. What encyclical remains as the basic authoritative analysis of the liturgy?
4. How does Art. 2 describe the Church?
5. What three events form the single paschal mystery?
6. What was the function of the apostles in the Church?
7. How is the liturgy a form of preaching Christ to which a new dimension of reality has been given by God?
8. How does the Church carry out the twofold function entrusted to the apostles?
9. How does the Church "complete" or "perfect" the work of salvation?
10. How does Art. 7 define liturgy?
11. Why is the liturgy the central activity of the Church?
12. Is full external participation in the liturgy an absolute condition for any form of participation whatsoever?
13. How does Art. 21 define the limits set to adaptation of the liturgy?
14. How does every Mass of itself have a public and social nature?
15. The liturgy is a celebration of the Word of God in which God speaks through Christ and the people respond to his invitation. Explain.

My Apostolate

1. The Constitution relies considerably on *Mediator Dei* and time and again it uses its very terminology, without quotation marks or reference. Needless to say, it would be to my advantage to read this great encyclical of Pius XII.
2. St. Paul's Epistle to the Hebrews describes most eloquently the eminent superiority of Christ's new dispensation over the old. I shall make an effort to study it.

2 The Holy Eucharist

Michael Myerscough, C.P.

DOCTRINAL AND PASTORAL INTRODUCTION
  (Arts. 47-49)

Article 47, the first article of chapter two, gives the doctrinal background for all that follows, the institution of the eucharistic sacrifice and Our Lord's command that it should be perpetuated "until he should come again"; his wish "to entrust . . . a memorial of his death and resurrection" to his Church; "a sacrament of love, a sign of unity, a bond of charity, a paschal banquet in which Christ is eaten, the mind is filled with a grace and a pledge of future glory is given to us."

This leads naturally into Art. 48, which begins: "The Church, therefore, earnestly desires that Christ's followers, when present at this mystery of faith, should not be there as strangers or silent spectators"—echoes of *Mediator Dei* and 1958 Instruction on Sacred Music and the Liturgy. With fine precision the part the people should play "in the sacred action" is here stated afresh—"they should take part . . . conscious of what they are doing, with devotion and full collaboration. They should be instructed by God's word (does this look forward to the provision for the vernacular in the readings mentioned in Art. 54?) and be nourished

49

at the table of the Lord's body." In Art. 55 it is strongly commended "that the faithful receive the Lord's body from the same sacrifice," in other words from hosts consecrated at the Mass they offer—in fact the article calls this practice "a more perfect form of participation in the Mass." Art. 48 continues that they should learn to offer themselves "by offering the immaculate victim not only through the hands of the priest, but also with him"; "through Christ their Mediator, they should be drawn day by day into ever more perfect union with God and with each other, so that finally God may be all in all."

"For this reason," Art. 49 states, "the Sacred Council, having in mind those Masses which are celebrated with the assistance of the faithful, especially on Sundays and feasts of obligation, has made the following decisions in order that the sacrifice of the Mass, *even in the ritual forms of its celebration* (italics mine) may become pastorally efficacious to the fullest degree."

REVISION OF THE MASS RITE (Art. 50)

Now follows in Art. 50 the decision of the Fathers to revise the rite of the Mass, which is to be done "in such a way that the intrinsic nature and purpose of its several parts, as also the connection between them, may be more clearly manifested, and that devout and active participation by the people may be more easily achieved. For this purpose the rites are to be simplified, due care being taken to preserve their substance." This will be done in two main ways:

(1) by *discarding* those "elements which, with the passage of time, came to be duplicated, or were added with but little advantage";

(2) by *restoring* "other elements which have suffered injury through accidents of history." These are "to be restored to the vigor which they had in the days of the holy Fathers, as may seem useful or necessary." If one may make bold to say on what lines the post-conciliar Commission will work with regard to the two points above—and it will be left to a post-conciliar Commission to apply these principles in practice—one would instance perhaps the shortening of the Offertory rite with its accumulation of prayers, the omission of preparatory prayers at the foot of the altar, the so-called Last Gospel; and as regards restorations, Art. 53 instances one important change already "the Community Prayer" or "Prayer of the Faithful" which is to be restored on Sundays and holydays of obligation especially, and will find its proper place "after the Gospel with its homily." "By this prayer, in which the people are to take part, intercession will be made for Holy Church, for the civil authorities, for those oppressed by various needs, for all mankind and for the salvation of the entire world." Learned liturgists have employed themselves for some time in the study of the "Prayer of the Faithful" or "Community Prayer"—notably Professor Fischer of Trier, not to speak of Father Jungmann, and according to them it would take the form of a litany to be recited by priest and people in alternation after the "liturgy of the word," *i.e.* after the residual *Oremus* that now incongruously adorns the beginning of the Offertory. As Art. 53 indicates, it will include the causes and needs of the people present and may, in the opinion of experts, end with some form of *Confiteor,* to replace the one at the foot of the altar. According to Father Jungmann, this is the moment best

suited for the confession of sinfulness after having listened to the ideal image of a Christian given us by the words of Scripture and the sermon; and before the Sacrifice-Banquet in which we are to participate freed from sins and imperfections by the "absolution" and our act of contrition *in globo*.

BIBLE READING IN THE LITURGY (Arts. 51-53)

"The treasures of the Bible are to be opened up more lavishly, so that richer fare may be provided for the faithful at the table of God's word. In this way *a more representative portion of the holy Scriptures will be read to the people in the course of a prescribed number of years*" (Art. 51) (italics mine). Many had requested a greater variety in the lessons of the Mass in the form of a cycle of three years or more; the Council itself has not determined this but the post-conciliar Commission will be entrusted with the task. Biblical scholars had already drawn up specimen "cycles" before the advent of the Council, so the spade-work has been done already.

Homily: In the new Codex Rubricarum (1960) a rubric — n. 474 — was inserted in the rubrics of the missal to the effect that "after the Gospel, especially on Sundays and feasts of precept, a brief homily is to be given to the people according to circumstances." The Constitution re-enforces this to the extent that "at the Masses which are celebrated with the assistance of the people on Sundays and holydays of obligation it should not be omitted except for a serious reason." What is more important, this article tells us clearly what is its purpose and content: "By means of the homily the mysteries of the faith and the guiding principles of the Christian life are expounded during the

course of the liturgical year, from the sacred text";
and—what is perhaps more important still in this
context—"the homily, therefore, is to be highly
esteemed as part of the liturgy itself." Far from
being an interruption of the liturgical rite, the
homily or sermon forms an integral part of the
service of God's word. According to experts, the
structure of the fore-Mass or liturgy of the word is
such as to require preaching and exposition of the
faith—Epistle, Gospel, Sermon. Father McManus,
a theological expert at the Council, says this should
be the normal and usual development in which the
reading of God's word is incomplete without the
living message of the teaching Church. We shall
have to wait for more precise instructions on the
application of this principle, but the fact that this
article states that the homily "is to be highly esteemed as part of the liturgy itself," that the next
article (53) conjoins it with the Gospel—when it
states that the "Prayer of the Faithful" is to be
restored" after the Gospel with its homily" (*cf.* also
Art. 78 on Matrimony which "is normally to be
celebrated within the Mass, after the reading of
the Gospel and the homily, just before the Prayer
of the Faithful")—surely means that henceforth
there will be no extraneous matter between the
Gospel and its explanation. The homily "is a con-
tinuation of the word of God, a part of the herald-
ing (*kerygma*) of the salvation of mankind through
the Word become Flesh, not a catechetical instruction, a pep talk or a meditation on a pious subject
of the preacher's own choice." (REINHOLD, *Bringing the Mass to the People,* p. 55, Burns and Oates,
London, 1960.) A careful reading of Art. 52 indicates that the homily belongs *especially* on Sundays and holydays of obligation, which means that

it is at least permitted, if not desirable, at certain weekday Masses at which the people are present, *e.g.* in Lent. The practice of a brief homily in such circumstances has been tremendously beneficial in many countries, but is growing only slowly in Britain and Ireland.

VERNACULAR IN THE MASS (Art. 54)

The article begins: "In those Masses which are celebrated with the people, a suitable place may be allotted to their mother-tongue. This is to apply in the first place to the readings and Prayers of the Faithful, but also, as local conditions may warrant, to those items of the liturgy which pertain to the people, according to the principle laid down in Art. 36 of this Constitution."

Readers are referred to an article in *The Tablet* (11-1-1964) by Archbishop Grimshaw (member of the Council Commission on the Liturgy, president of a sub-commission of the same, and currently chairman of a body of English-speaking bishops for the vernacular texts that may be used in the Mass) on this still very much disputed question, the use of the mother-tongue. He makes the salient point that "the bishops of the universal Church have decided that changes must be made, but that these changes are not unlimited." Art. 36, states: "1: Though existing special exemptions are to remain in force, the use of the Latin language is to be preserved in the Latin rites. 2: But since the use of the mother-tongue is frequently of great advantage to the people in the Mass . . . the limits of its employment may be extended. This will apply in the first place to the readings and directives, and to some of the prayers and chants, according to the regulations on this matter to be laid down sepa-

rately in subsequent chapters. 3: These norms
being observed, it is for the competent ecclesiastical
authority, mentioned in Art. 22, §2, to decide
whether and to what extent, the vernacular language is to be used; their decrees are to be approved, that is, confirmed, by the Holy See. And
whenever it seems to be called for, they are to consult with the bishops of neighboring territories
which have the same language. 4: Translations
from the Latin text intended for use in the liturgy
must be approved by the competent local authority
mentioned above."

Art. 36 thus gives to "various kinds of local
bishops' conferences" (*cf.* Art. 22, §2) the power to
decide, within the limits of the Constitution, how
the vernacular should be used, only seeking confirmation of their decisions from the Holy See;
and secondly the same bodies have the power to ap-
prove the vernacular texts to be used. It will belong
to the local bishops' conferences to determine as
soon as possible (according to Bishop Jenny, Auxiliary of Cambrai, in an article in *Informations Cath-
oliques Internationales,* Dec. 15, 1963) what texts
recited or sung of the Ordinary of the Mass are "to
be translated and used in the living language of the
people" in addition to the Epistle and Gospel and
the "Prayer of the Faithful." For sung Masses it
seems obvious that the *Kyrie, Gloria,* etc. will be in
Latin everywhere until such time as there will be a
wedding between approved translations and sufficiently beautiful melodies if and when desired. Indeed it would appear almost impossible to achieve
this until the Missal is revised after the Council.
Also, Art. 54, after the paragraph on the use of the
vernacular at Mass, states: "Nevertheless steps must
be taken to insure that the faithful are able to say

or sing together, also in Latin, those parts of the Ordinary of the Mass which are rightfully theirs."

Art. 54 concludes with a very telling paragraph: "If an even more extended use of the mother-tongue within the Mass appears desirable in some parts of the world, the procedure laid down in Art. 40 of this Constitution is to be observed." In brief, it means, according to Archbishop Grimshaw, that if changes are desired in those parts of the Mass recited or sung by the priest, the local episcopal conferences must present their suggestions to the Holy See for approval—the new formula granting legislative power to the local bishops was not introduced into Art. 40. He says: "Our present Art. 54, must be read particularly carefully insofar as it concerns the part of the Mass which the priest says or sings." If, for example, it was desired to have the Collect and Post-Communion in the vernacular then the means provided in Art. 40 would have to be used. For the chants of the Proper of the Mass—Antiphons for the *Introit* etc.—Bishop Jenny thinks it possible that the permission will be given to use an approved translation, but "the big difficulty here at present consists in employing a form of music which at one and the same time matches up the living language to the dignity of the sacred text."

Apart from sung Masses, this has added weight when considering dialogue Masses at which hymns or psalms are sung at the beginning, at the Offertory, Communion and the end of Mass, as is done fairly frequently nowadays. One wonders how many people would prefer to recite vernacular texts at this time? Some think it would be a good idea to use an existing translation (if approved) against the time—5 to 7 years hence—when the Missal will have been revised. To summarize the provisions of Art. 54 regarding the introduction of the vernacular:

(1) For those parts recited or sung by the people, in addition to the readings and the "Prayer of the Faithful" (*oratio communis*), the decision rests with the local bishops' conferences.

(2) For those parts recited or sung by the priest —*cf*. Art. 40—those wishing to introduce changes here must present their suggestions to the Holy See for approval, *e.g.* Collect and Post-Communion.

COMMUNION UNDER BOTH KINDS (Art. 55)

After confirming "the dogmatic principles about communion of the faithful which were laid down by the Council of Trent" (communion "under one kind alone") the article goes on to enumerate the occasions on which "communion under both species may be granted when the bishops think fit, not only to clerics and religious, but also to the laity, in certain cases to be determined by the Apostolic See—as for instance, to the newly-ordained in their Mass of Ordination, to the newly-professed in their Mass of religious profession, and to the newly-baptized in the Mass which follows their baptism."

The restoration of the chalice to the laity in these special circumstances will be most welcome to all who have the true reform of the liturgy at heart but it will take some time to bring it into orderly practice, whereas it is relatively easy to introduce the faithful to receiving Holy Communion with hosts consecrated at the same sacrifice—"a more perfect form of participation in the Mass" the Constitution calls it.

ONE SINGLE ACT OF WORSHIP (Art. 56)

"The two parts which, in a certain sense, go to make up the Mass, namely the liturgy of the word and the eucharistic liturgy, are so closely connected with each other that they form but one single act of worship." Pastors of souls are therefore strongly urged to instruct their people "to take their part in the entire Mass, especially on Sundays and holydays of obligation." One fervently hopes that more and more people will come to realize the truth proclaimed here—"the intimate link between the Word and the Sacrament"—concerning which there has been much study among liturgists in recent years. (*Cf.* French Liturgical Week, Strasbourg, in 1957.) "These studies show greater affinity between the two parts of the Mass than was suspected by the preceding generations of pure historians. It would be a mistake nowadays to attach importance to the 'historical accident theory' by which a fusion took place of the synagogal service (reading and praying) with the new mystery of the Breaking of the Bread." (REINHOLD, op. cit., p. 51.) Father Reinhold summarizes the truth when he says: "as Jesus was physically present at the Last Supper, so he is present in his Word during the Fore-Mass." (ibid.)

A true appreciation of this point by priests themselves should lead to a favorable response by their people. One hopes, now that the homily is to be restored to its rightful place, followed by the Prayer of the Faithful, that notices and announcements will be reduced to a minimum, and will not descend to the sort of announcements that could be carried in parish bulletins and magazines.

CONCELEBRATION (Arts. 57-58)

"Concelebration, whereby the unity of the priesthood is appropriately manifested, has remained in use to this day in the Church both eastern and western. For this reason it has seemed good to the Council to extend permission for concelebration to the following cases." (Art. 57 §1.)

The decision of the Council to commend and extend concelebration in well-determined cases, is in line with the principle outlined in Art. 27, that "whenever rites, according to their specific nature, make provision for *communal celebration* involving the presence and active participation of the people, this way of celebrating them is to be preferred— so far as possible—to a celebration that is individual and quasi-private. This applies with especial force to the celebration of Mass . . . even though every Mass has of itself a public and social nature." On this last point, Art. 57 §2 having said that "it is for the bishop, however, to regulate the discipline of concelebration in the diocese," goes on to add, "but each priest shall always retain his right to celebrate Mass individually, though not at the same time in the same church as a concelebrated Mass, nor on Holy Thursday."

We are familiar with concelebration at Ordination Masses, and when a bishop is consecrated. The permission for it is now extended to Holy Thursday (both the Chrism Mass and the Evening Mass), to Masses during councils, bishops' conferences and synods, and at the Mass for the blessing of an abbot. The next section of Art. 57, §1 (ii), continues: "also with permission of the Ordinary to whom it belongs to decide whether concelebration is opportune, and to regulate the way in which it is done:

(a) At conventual Mass, and at the principal Mass in churches when the needs of the faithful do not require that all priests available should celebrate individually.

(b) At Masses celebrated at any kind of priests' meetings whether the priests be secular clergy or religious."

We shall all need to do much re-thinking of our ideas before the idea of concelebration and its practice take deep root. Our starting point and indeed "the point of no return" will be the Council's own words that by concelebration "the unity of the priesthood is appropriately manifested." Most priests will be grateful for the extension of permissions: may we live to see concelebration in practice! It would seem still to be a thing of the future, for as Art. 58 decrees—"a new rite for concelebration is to be drawn up and inserted into the Pontifical and into the Roman Missal."

Discussion Questions

1. According to Art. 47, why did Christ institute the eucharistic sacrifice of his body and blood?
2. By what twofold manner are the liturgical rites to be simplified?
3. What does Art. 52 tell us about the purpose and content of the homily?
4. Since the homily is to be esteemed as "part of the liturgy itself," would you prefer one at every Mass?
5. What does Art. 36 tell us about the use of the vernacular in the Mass?
6. What do you think about the restoration of the chalice to the laity (communion under both kinds)?
7. How is the Mass one single act of worship?
8. What is concelebration?

My Apostolate

1. Since the Church desires that the faithful "when present at this mystery of faith, should not be there as strangers or silent spectators," I will remember to take part in the sacrificial banquet as actively as possible, conscious of what is going on, together with devotion and full collaboration.
2. In the words of Fr. Reinhold, "as Jesus was physically present at the Last Supper, so he is present in his Word during the Fore-Mass." In other words there is an intimate link between Word and Sacrament, between the liturgy of the word and the eucharistic liturgy. A true appreciation of this truth will encourage me to participate in the entire Mass.

3 Sacraments and Sacramentals

Liam Walsh, O.P.

In the language of the Church a "constitution" is a document that is at once doctrinal and disciplinary: it teaches dogmatic truth and lays down related rules of action. The schema on the liturgy was drafted by the preparatory commission as a constitution. It was proposed that the practical program of reform should be shown to follow from the very nature and purpose of the liturgy. The Fathers of the Council approved this style and method, and it remains in the text which they eventually ratified. The chapter on the sacraments and sacramentals is a good example of it. The relevant doctrinal principles are set down in n. 59-61. A transition from the theoretical to the practical occurs in n. 62, and the disciplinary principles of reform follow, n. 63-82.

DOCTRINE

The title of the chapter is interesting: "Of the *other* sacraments and the sacramentals." The previous chapter has dealt with "The mystery of the Holy Eucharist," that is to say, with the Mass. The Mass is the center of the sacramental system: it is itself a sacrament, and it holds all the other sacraments together in a balanced unity. So, once it has dealt with the Mass, including Communion, the Council proceeds to discuss the remainder of the sacramental system, namely, "The other sacraments and the sacramentals." This stress on the comprehensive unity of the sacramental order, with the Mass as its center, is characteristic of the Constitution. Trent had to break down the sacramental system into its component parts; it had to define the number of sacraments, and to analyze the specific nature of each; it had to set forth clearly the special position of the Mass as a sacrifice. Vatican II is able to return to a more synthetic view of the liturgy.[1]

PURPOSE OF THE SACRAMENTS (Art. 59)

The text begins by expressing the purpose of the sacraments in three phases: "to sanctify men, to build up the body of Christ and finally to give worship to God." The first phase, the sanctification of men, we can understand readily enough. We learned in our catechism that the sacraments are sources, causes of sanctifying grace. But perhaps our catechism did not take us much further. Perhaps we were left with the impression that the sacraments were private sources of supply, personal preserves, to which "I had recourse" for the good of *my soul*. The Council is not satisfied with this sacramental individualism. The sacraments, it goes on, "build up the body of Christ." It is in the Church, with the Church and by the Church that

---

[1] Father F. Antonelli, O.F.M., secretary of the conciliar commission on the liturgy notes the complementary character of Trent and Vatican II in an article in *L'Osservatore Romano* (Dec. 8, 1963).

I am sanctified. It is the Church which offers me the sacraments and by them she draws me into her social life as the body of Christ. And this membership of the Church leads to the third phase in the purpose of the sacraments, "to give worship to God." We are sanctified for worship. All creation is directed to the glory of God. Free, responsible creatures have to be specially directed. They must be sanctified, set apart by grace for God, if they are to promote his glory. And because men are social creatures they are sanctified in a community, for community worship. They become "a kingly priesthood and a holy nation" (Exod. 19, 6). It is this third phase which gives a properly liturgical dimension to the sacramental system.

It is not an unjust criticism to say that post-tridentine sacramental instruction has hardly done justice to the worship value of the sacraments. It expounded admirably their sanctifying efficacy, that downward movement by which grace comes from God to the soul, through the intrinsic power of a validly celebrated sacrament. But it tended to see the upward movement of worship only in the sacrificial aspect of the Mass. Perhaps part of the difficulty came from a rather legalistic habit of reducing the sacraments to their essential "matter and form," and from a preoccupation with the validity of a celebration rather than with its integrity. There is more to the sacraments than valid matter and form. The Church has designed a full ritual setting around the essential centerpiece, in which there is a constant elevation of the mind to God in praise, thanksgiving, petition, self-oblation—all the upsurge of Christian worship in spirit and in truth. The sacraments are acts of worship because they are each related to the Mass;

and through the Mass they share in the paschal mystery of Christ. Even the laws of their celebration show them gravitating toward the Mass. Baptism and confirmation are stages in a rite of Christian initiation that reaches its climax in the eucharist. Penance restores one to eucharistic communion. Anointing of the sick is, when possible, completed by Communion or Viaticum. Orders and matrimony take place, ideally, within Mass itself. As well as that, baptism, confirmation and orders produce a sacramental character, which is a consecration of men, in varying degrees, for the celebration of eucharistic worship.

SIGNS (ibid.)

The opening sentence of the chapter continues, "because they are signs they also instruct." The sacraments are signs: this is a key principle for understanding their nature and purpose.[2] It is as signs that they achieve their triple purpose already mentioned by the Council: they signify the special sanctifying grace which they cause; they are social signs which build up and manifest the unity of the body of Christ; they are external signs such as are required by the very nature of human worship. The Council takes all this for granted in its phrasing and punctuation of this opening sentence. What it is more concerned to stress is that because the sacraments are signs they must *instruct*. A sign is an aid to knowledge, it helps the mind to identify things and to communicate with other minds. And because the sacraments are signs of supernat-

---

[2] It is the first thing established by St. Thomas in his treatment of the sacraments, III, q. 60. The idea of sign has already been introduced by the Council in n. 33.

ural realities, they speak, not just for our reason, but for our faith. The Council puts it this way: "They not only presuppose faith, but by words and objects they also nourish, strengthen and express it; that is why they are called 'sacraments of faith'." There are two aspects of the activity of faith mentioned here. We understand the first readily enough: the sacraments presuppose the faith of the Church, and of the person for whom they are celebrated. But the second aspect is, perhaps, less familiar to us: the sacraments cause and express faith. The words of the ritual (scriptural texts and prayers) and the material elements employed *mean* something. That is precisely why Christ chose them and why the Church developed them. Our faith reads that meaning and, "in the very act of celebrating" it is instructed and comes alive. The Council of Trent insisted strongly that the faithful were to be instructed in the meaning of the ritual of Mass and the sacraments, so that they could enter more fully into the celebration. In spite of that it would seem that subsequently more attention was paid to the causality of the sacraments than to their value as instructive signs. More stress was put on the intrinsic power of the rite, especially of its essential matter and form, to cause grace *ex opere operato* than on its value as an exercise of personal faith. The sacraments tended to be seen as *things* which did something, rather than as instruments of an immediate encounter between God and ourselves, in which we were sanctified and God was worshipped. True we have always been instructed to dispose ourselves properly for the sacraments, to prepare ourselves by faith, charity and a right intention. But perhaps we regarded that preparation as somewhat extrinsic to the sacrament itself, something to be done beforehand rather than throughout, and by means of the entire ritual of the sacrament. Take the hypothetical example of a priest who would spend a quarter of an hour in fervent preparation for Mass and then "fly" uncomprehendingly through the Mass itself, satisfied that his rubrics were correct and that his consecration was valid. Such a celebration would, indeed, give worship to God and make grace available to men. But insofar as it was a routine ritual rather than a living dialogue of faith it would do little or nothing to enlighten and form those dispositions on which the fruitfulness of the sacrament depends. It is this power of "the very act of celebrating" to cause dispositions of faith, worship and love that the Council wants to stress: "They have indeed the power to impart grace, but, in addition, the very act of celebrating them effectively disposes the faithful to receive this grace fruitfully, to worship God duly and to love each other mutually."

The practical conclusion which is drawn from the doctrine of the first paragraph is an exact statement of the program of what is nowadays called Pastoral Liturgy: "Firstly, it is therefore of the highest importance that the faithful should easily understand the sacramental signs." They will understand the sacraments easily if they have that "noble simplicity" which the Council desires to see in the restored liturgy (n. 34); if they are properly carried out by the minister (n. 18); and if they are explained—although they "normally should not require much explanation" (n. 34). If the faithful understand the sacraments they will be more likely to carry out the second part of the program, which is that they "should frequent with great eagerness those sacraments which were instituted to nourish the Christian life." They will frequent the sacraments, not simply out of a sense of obligation or because of social pressures but willingly and joyfully.

SACRAMENTALS (Arts. 60-61)

Christ instituted sacraments, to which he gave an intrinsic power of signifying and producing special effects, in his name. The Church cannot, of course, institute new sacraments. But she can do something analogous. In her own name she chooses certain symbolical objects or actions, which the blesses or consecrates with prayer. She offers these "sacramentals" to the faithful as signs of special graces which they can receive through the intercession of the Church. By the sacramentals "various occasions in daily life are rendered holy." But more than that—and this is something we do not always advert to in our devotions—"by their aid men are disposed to receive the chief fruits of the sacraments." This gets us back again to the cardinal principle of the unity of the sacramental system. Although the sacramentals are infinitely beneath the sacraments as sources of grace they play their humble part in one great dispensation. Many of them are used in the sacraments themselves or are derived from them. But wherever they occur they are part of the liturgy. They help to maintain, all through life, that contact with the sacred which reaches its periodic climax in the sacraments. As the Council puts it, the faithful "are given access to the stream of divine grace which flows from the paschal mystery of the passion, death and resurrection of Christ, the fount from which all the sacraments and sacramentals draw their power " The

Council does not enter into the thorny question of *how* the sacramental system makes the paschal mystery of salvation available to us. But it does state the wonderful fact that the mystery of Christ is active in the liturgy, radiating grace into every moment of our lives, sanctifying our actions and consecrating them to worship. Through the sacraments and sacramentals "there is hardly any proper use of material things which cannot thus be directed toward the sanctification of men and the praise of God."

DISCIPLINE (Art. 62)

The Council has already explained that the liturgy contains some elements that are unchangeable, because divinely instituted, and others that are human additions that may come and go with the tide of history (n. 21). Liturgical studies over the past half-century have made it possible to distinguish the permanent core of the sacraments from the accessory developments. They have also shown that some of the accessories have tended to obscure the meaning of the sacraments themselves, especially for the people of our own time. The Council candidly makes this criticism its own: "With the passage of time, however, there have crept into the rites of the sacraments and sacramentals certain features which have rendered their nature and purpose far from clear to the people of today." And since its stated purpose is to make the sacraments as understandable and accessible as they are meant to be by their very nature "some changes have become necessary to adapt them to the needs of our own times." For this reason the Council "decrees as follows concerning their revision." The decrees which follow deal with each of the sacraments and with some of the sacramentals. However, they are general principles of reform rather than concrete proposals. The details of reform remain to be worked out by what are being called "post-conciliar commissions." In commenting on the text, therefore, we have to remain on a rather general level, with an occasional tentative suggestion by way of illustration.

VERNACULAR RITUAL (Art. 63)

The general principles governing the use of the language of the people in the liturgy have already been laid down (n. 36). They apply without further restriction to the sacraments. One gathers that there was a proposal to insist here that the essential form of the sacraments should remain in Latin. If so it was not accepted by the Council. If the form is to remain in Latin it will be at the discretion of the bishops, not at the command of the Council.

The liturgical book which regulates the administration of the sacraments and sacramentals by priests is the Ritual. The prototype of Latin rituals is the *Rituale Romanum,* published under Paul V in 1614. Although it was not imposed on all the Latin Churches, as were other Roman liturgical books, it gradually came into general use. The *Rituale* itself allowed that it could be adapted to local customs and needs, but it was not until about 1930 that advantage came to be taken of this permission on any notable scale. The Holy See began to allow various hierarchies, especially in missionary countries, to use supplements, or appendices to the Roman Ritual. In these the vernacular was introduced in varying degrees, and adaptations were made in the ritual of the sacraments.[3]

What was formerly a concession becomes a command in the Council. Regional ecclesiastical authorities are told to "prepare without delay local rituals adapted, also as regards the language employed, to local needs." The Holy See, for its part, promises a new edition of the Roman Ritual. The new local rituals will, on the one hand, be harmonized with this Roman Ritual, and on the other hand adapted to local conditions. Once they have been approved by the Holy See they must be "introduced into the localities for which they have been prepared." The Council shows once again how preoccupied it is with making the sacraments understood and pastorally effective when it adds: "In the Roman Ritual each one of the rites is preceded by an instruction, pastoral or rubrical in nature, or referring to the social importance of the rite. These introductions are not to be omitted from the particular rituals or collections of rites which are to be drawn up." Presumably it wants priests who use the Ritual to have these instructions at their fingertips so that their administration of the sacraments will not just be an exercise in rubrical etiquette, but a meaningful action, both for themselves and for the community of the faithful.

BAPTISM (Arts. 64-70)

In this missionary age adult baptism is no longer the exception it was during the ages of faith. So the Council re-introduces the catechumenate for

---

[3] Such a new ritual came into use in Ireland, for instance, in 1961.

adults. At present an adult prepares for baptism by an intensive course of instruction in catechism. This is not meant to be a kind of cramming, as for an exam. It is part of a religious process, which should prepare the entire person, morally and spiritually as well as intellectually, to adhere to Christ and to enter into the paschal ‹mystery. So it is fitting that the progress of the convert's preparation should be marked by liturgical ceremony, as it was in the early centuries of the Church. "By this means the time of the catechumenate, which is intended as a period of suitable instruction (*institutio*) may be sanctified by sacred rites to be celebrated after successive intervals of time." Presumably the new catechumenate will be inspired by the ancient practice of the *Scrutinia* which were held at various days during Lent in preparation for Easter baptism. The gradual advance of the catechumen's instruction, and his progressive liberation from the devil, his works and his pomps, will be sanctified by means of prayer and sacramentals, including exorcisms. His sense of reliance on God and the mercy of the Church rather than on his own efforts will be intensified in preparation for the grace of baptism.

There is obvious scope for adaptation to local custom here. The Council notes that "In mission territories it is found that some of the peoples already make use of initiation rites." These are colorful ceremonies which symbolize that, for instance, an infant is received into the tribal community, or young people are promoted from childhood to the adult state. While these rites are, to all appearances, pagan they may have elements of genuine religious value; and they always have a powerful psychological and symbolical force for the people who practice them. Provided they are "not indissolubly bound up with superstition and error" (n. 37) they may be admitted to the ceremonies of Christian initiation.[4]

The ritual of baptism itself is to be revised. The existing rites, those for adults and for infants, are of a rather "makeshift" historical derivation. The Council wants the different rites reconstructed so that they will be more realistically adapted to their purpose. That for adults is to take the restored catechumenate into account; that for infants is to treat them as infants, and give more prominence to the roles and duties of godparents and parents; and there should be variants that would make the baptism of many people together more practicable. There is also to be a shorter rite "for use chiefly by catechists in mission territories, but also by the faithful in general when there is danger of death, yet neither priest nor deacon is available." This will surround the essential matter and form of baptism, which is all that is said and done nowadays in such an emergency, with a certain minimum of solemnity and ceremonial.

When an infant who is baptized by the "short form" survives, the Church requires that all the ceremonies of baptism should be administered in due course. They are valuable sacramentals, and also help to express the public nature of baptism. At present the ceremony is the same as a full baptism, except that the matter and form is omitted. Obviously there is a certain artificiality about this: a child who is already baptized cannot, except by some legal fiction, be received as if it were still a

4 For examples of these rites and possible adaptations cf Liturgy and the Missions, edited by J. Hofinger, S.J., Burns and Oates, 1960, pp. 209 sq.

pagan. So the Council, anxious that everything
in the liturgy should be realistic and meaningful,
asks for a new rite that would "manifest more
fittingly and clearly that the infant, baptized by
the short rite, has already been received into the
Church." It also wants a new rite "for converts
who have already been validly baptized; it should
indicate that they are now admitted to communion
with the Church," for this is the positive purpose
of the rite.

Finally we must note a significant prescription:
"A special Mass 'For the Conferring of Baptism'
is to be inserted into the Roman Missal." This is
a practical expression of the principle that the
Mass is the keystone of the sacramental edifice.
The meaning of all the sacraments is clearer when
they are celebrated in association with it. Baptism
is particularly enhanced, because the Christian
initiation begun in it finds its fulfillment in the
eucharist.

CONFIRMATION (Art. 71)

There has been a good deal of discussion about
the sacrament of confirmation in recent years. At-
tempts have been made to relate it to Catholic
Action and various other obligations of the adult
Catholic life. The age at which it should be administered has been particularly debated. In fact
there has been considerable variation in the discipline of the Church over the centuries. Nowadays the Code of Canon Law mentions the "fit-
tingness" of the present practice which "delays"
the sacrament until the age of seven, but allows
that it may be administered to infants in danger
of death. Yet it is common practice to delay it
until well after the age of seven, and to administer

it after First Communion. The Council does not enter into these problems, but it does lay down an important principle about the nature of confirmation which should appear in the new rite: "the intimate connection which this sacrament has with the whole process of Christian initiation is to be more clearly set forth." Initiation into the Christian life is not simply a matter of signing a document; nor is it merely a moral decision to be converted. Ideally it is a progressive sacramental celebration, comprising baptism, confirmation and eucharist, in that order, as well as many associated sacramentals. The present ritual of confirmation makes the proper effects of the sacrament quite clear, but does not sufficiently show how these effects fit into the complete process of initiation. The Council mentions the renewal of baptismal vows before confirmation as a way in which the connection with baptism could be expressed. It also allows confirmation to be given within Mass, which would help to show how confirmation prepares for the eucharist.

PENANCE (Art. 72)

Here too the Council asks for a revised rite that will "more clearly express both the nature and effects of the sacrament." Possibly it is thinking especially of the social nature and effects of penance. The present ritual is highly individualistic and private. It hardly does justice to the fact that penance reconciles us to the Church as well as to God, and restores us to full eucharistic communion.

ANOINTING OF THE SICK (Art. 73-75)

It is always difficult to change a well-established

name by a peremptory law. The Council wisely allows a gradual transition from "extreme unction" to "anointing of the sick." It admits both names but states its preference for the latter and, one assumes, hopes it will eventually prevail. There is more to the change than a matter of language. "Extreme unction" suggests a sacrament that is administered to people *in extremis*. In our own time people rarely "send for the priest" until the very last moment, when most human hope is gone. In fact this sacrament is meant for the sick, not just for the dying. (They must of course be seriously ill "through old age or infirmity" and, to that extent, "in danger of death.") The sacrament is meant to give them spiritual strength in their illness and to restore their bodily health. It is so much more effective if the patient is conscious and well enough to take an active part in the ceremony. To increase the realism of the rite, and to allow for various degrees of participation, the Council orders that "The number of anointings is to be adapted to the occasion and the prayers which accompany the anointings are to be revised so as to correspond with the varying conditions of the sick who receive the sacrament."

Viaticum is, more properly, the sacrament of the dying, their last eucharistic nourishment on the road to eternity. It may be given apart from anointing, but for cases when the two sacraments are given together "a continuous rite is to be prepared in which the sick man is anointed after he has made his confession and before he receives viaticum." In the present ritual, as a result of various historical accidents, viaticum is given before anointing. The revised order is more in keeping with the nature and effects of the two sacraments and expresses once again the culminating place of the eucharist in the sacramental system.[5]

ORDINATIONS (Art. 76)

The Council wants a revision of the rites and prayers of ordination. The call for the vernacular will not be so urgent here, as the sacrament principally concerns clerics. But "The address given by the bishop at the beginning of each ordination or consecration may be in the mother tongue." This address is a paternal exhortation to those being ordained. It could be less rigid and more touching if spoken in the vernacular. Before ordination to the priesthood there is also an address directed to the clergy and faithful who are present. Perhaps the revised rite will direct itself more often in this way to the assembled community, which is, after all, deeply interested in those who are being ordained to minister to it. In that case a greater use of the vernacular would be called for.

At present, in the consecration of a bishop, only the consecrating prelate and his two co-consecrators perform the central act, the laying on of hands. In the future all the bishops present may do so. This is a return to ancient discipline. Perhaps it is intended as a ritual expression of the collegiality of bishops, and their right to join actively in admitting a new brother-bishop to their ranks.

MARRIAGE (Arts. 77-78)

Not alone must the ritual of marriage be revised, it must be "enriched"—a kindly thought for this

---

[5] This order has already been adopted in, for instance, the new German Ritual. It has always been maintained in the Dominican Rite.

loveliest of sacraments. It is, of course, a spiritual enrichment that the Council is thinking of, "in such a way that the grace of the sacrament is more clearly signified and the duties of the spouses are impressed upon them." Since the Council of Trent there has always been a good deal of local liberty about the ritual of marriage. The prescription of Trent on the subject is quoted with approval here. But Vatican II goes even further: "the competent ecclesiastical authority . . . is free to devise its own rite suited to place and people," subject to the limitations already mentioned about incorporating local practices into the liturgy. But in such new ceremonials there must be no interference with the essential law of marriage, which is "that the priest assisting at the marriage must ask for and obtain the consent of the contracting parties."

Marriage, like the other sacraments, is to be closely related to the Mass. It is normally to be cele- brated within the Mass, after the reading of the Gospel and the homily just before the "Prayer of the Faithful." The Nuptial Mass will include a re- vised form of the Prayer for the Bride (the prayer said by the priest after the *Pater Noster* of the Mass). At present the wishes and warnings of this prayer are directed mainly to the bride. The re- vised prayer will bring the groom more into the picture. It may be said in the vernacular and "will remind both spouses of their equal obligations to remain faithful to each other." If marriage has to be celebrated outside Mass the Council orders that at least "the Epistle and Gospel from the Nuptial Mass are to read as an introduction to the cere- mony, and the spouses should always be given a blessing." At present the Nuptial Blessing is not given at certain times and circumstances, nor is it

ever given outside Mass. In the future there will
be no such restrictions.

THE SACRAMENTALS (Art. 79)

The prescriptions here are rather general: There
is to be "a revision which takes into account the
basic principles for enabling the faithful to participate intelligently, actively and easily." Such participation will protect the faithful from all shades
of superstition in their use of the sacramentals. "It
is lawful even to add new sacramentals as the need
for these becomes apparent." This could be done
in mission territories. New sacramentals might also
help to sanctify modern technological civilization
as the older ones sanctified rural life. "Reserved
blessings shall be very few . . . in favor only of
bishops or ordinaries." Thus, it seems, priests of
certain religious orders will lose the proprietary
right they have at present to certain blessings.
Some sacramentals may, with due safeguards "be
administered by suitably qualified lay persons."
One might imagine, for example, some sacramentals associated with admission to the lay apostolate
being administered by lay leaders.

RELIGIOUS PROFESSION (Art. 80)

Profession is an act of religion that enters closely
into the general framework of the liturgy. The
Council calls for certain revisions in the rites. The
Solemn Consecration of Virgins, a rite proper to
some monastic orders of nuns, is to be revised.
Presumably it will give clearer expression to the
Church's doctrine on virginity, which is an im-
portant counterbalance to the teaching on marriage.

The ordinary rites of religious profession are at present as varied, and sometimes as fanciful, as the religious habits of monks and nuns. A special rite is to be drawn up, in the interests of "uniformity (*unitas*), moderation and dignity," which must be used "by those who make their profession or renovation of vows during Mass." Religious profession does not have to be made during Mass, but the Council expressly recommends that it should. The religious and sacrificial meaning of profession is powerfully emphasized when, for instance, it is made at the Offertory of the Mass. The common practice of having at least Benediction after the ceremony of profession shows the instinctive eucharistic tendency of profession. Mass would express it even more perfectly, and the unity of the liturgical life around the altar would, once again, be stressed.[6]

BURIAL RITES (Arts. 81-82)

The natural gloom of mourning has tended at times to stifle the joyful hope of resurrection which belonged originally to the funeral rites of the Church. The paschal color of white, for instance, gave way to somber black, the *Alleluia* (still found in the eastern rites) to the *Dies Irae*. The Council wants the joy of the resurrection brought back to prominence in the rite. It "should express more clearly the paschal character of Christian death."[7] Local traditions and customs are to be taken into account, notably in the matter of liturgical colors.

[6] Cf. Rule of St. Benedict, c. 58.

[7] See E. H. Schillebeeckx, O.P., "The Death of a Christian" in *Vatican II: A Struggle of Minds*, Gill and Son, Dublin, 1963.

In Africa, for instance, the color of mourning is not black but red. A new burial rite for infants is to be devised—the present one is simply an adaptation of that used for adults—and a special Mass is to be provided for the occasion.

Discussion Questions

1. In the language of the Church, what is a "constitution"?
2. What is the purpose of the sacraments?
3. Why are the sacraments acts of worship?
4. It is as signs that the sacraments achieve their triple purpose. Explain.
5. What are sacramentals?
6. What is the purpose of sacramentals?
7. What is the catechumenate for adults?
8. How is initiation into the Christian life a progressive sacramental celebration comprising baptism, confirmation and the eucharist?
9. What do Arts. 73-75 say about the anointing of the sick?
10. Why should the sacrament of marriage be celebrated within the Mass?
11. Can you mention some sacramentals that might be administered by the laity?
12. What has this chapter added to your understanding of the comprehensive unity of the sacramental order?

My Apostolate

1. Each time I receive a sacrament worthily, I will remember that I am sanctifying myself, building up the body of Christ and giving worship to God.
2. Sacramentals help us to maintain, all through life, that contact with the sacred which reaches its periodic climax in the sacraments. I shall use them more often.

4 The Divine Office

Vincent Ryan, O.S.B.

INSTEAD of treating successively of all nineteen articles of this chapter, I propose to group the matter in logical order under five general headings: (1) Doctrine; (2) The rhythm of liturgical prayer; (3) The content of the new office; (4) Communal celebration; (5) The vernacular.

DOCTRINE

With regard to the theology of the divine office, Articles 83-87 of this chapter are a faithful echo of *Mediator Dei*.[1] The teaching of Pope Pius XII on the dignity and supreme value of liturgical prayer is here reaffirmed. The pre-eminence of the divine office derives from the fact that it is the prayer of the whole Christ, head and members: "It is the very prayer which Christ himself, together with his body, addresses to the Father" (Art. 84).

Art. 86 of this chapter disposes of the notion that the divine office should be relegated to the background of pastoral life. On the contrary, it is those priests who are most absorbed in pastoral and apostolic work who will have most need of prayer. No amount of missionary activity will bear fruit

[1] Cf. London CTS edition, nn. 146-153.

unless it is sustained by a life of prayer, and no prayer is more efficacious than that spoken by the Church in the sacred liturgy.

The purpose of the new reforms becomes perfectly clear after a careful reading of this chapter. It is not the intention of the Council to curtail liturgical prayer through any lessening of esteem for the divine office, but, rather, to infuse new life into it and to adapt it to the conditions of modern life: "not less prayer, but better prayer."

The Council in formulating these decrees was obviously motivated by a deep concern for *truth,* a desire to see the Church's official worship conforming to the norms of authenticity and sincerity. The off-hand manner with which, in the past, we may have satisfied our obligation to the divine office will no longer be considered good enough. There will no longer be any excuse for simply "getting in" our office at any hour of the day or night, for telescoping the different periods of prayer, nor for the hundred-and-one other anomalies which formerly we took for granted.

The divine office must now become a personal, conscious and deeply interior prayer, in which mind and voice are in perfect harmony (Art. 90). It must become the authentic expression of the personal piety of its minister—priest or religious. In order that this inner harmony be realized, there will be a need for all to acquire a solid biblical culture, and, especially, an understanding of, and relish for, the psalms.

A final characteristic doctrinal feature of this chapter is the manifest importance accorded to communal celebration of the divine office. The superiority of choral, or common, celebration over solitary celebration of the office is based on the fact that the former better manifests the essentially communal character of liturgical prayer. But we must always bear in mind that the divine office, even when celebrated in private, is, of its nature, the prayer of the society of Christians joined to Christ.

THE RHYTHM OF LITURGICAL PRAYER

In response to Christ's exhortation that we pray at all times, the Church has, in the course of the ages, instituted the different liturgical hours. The purpose of these, as Art. 88 points out, is to sanctify the Christian day; and the Council expresses the desire that the traditional sequence of the hours be restored so that they may be truly related to the time of the day when they are prayed. It recognizes, however, the difficulty of putting this principle into practice under modern conditions and the accelerated tempo of living. Our actual method of marking the hours of day and night differs greatly from the old Roman system which divided the night into four vigils and the day into four "hours," viz., *prima, tertia, sexta,* and *nona;* it is from these that our "small hours" have derived their names.

A more practical horarium has been drawn up which will enable even the busiest priest to follow the traditional order of hours. Art. 89 lays down the main principles of this reform. First, it declares that Lauds and Vespers being, respectively, the morning and evening prayers of the Church, are to be considered the basic hours of the office, "the two hinges on which the daily office turns." This is a return to authentic tradition. Morning and evening will always form the natural divisions of the day. They have always been times specially consecrated to prayer, and from as early as the third century they had a liturgical office assigned to them. Moreover, from earliest times, the hours of Lauds and Vespers had a distinctly public character about them; of their very nature they call for the participation of the faithful. It is for this reason that, further on (Art. 100), the Constitution exhorts parish priests to celebrate these hours in common with the faithful in church on Sundays and on the more solemn feasts.

Compline is the prayer to be said before retiring; hence "it is to be drawn up so that it will be a suitable prayer for the end of the day." This seems to mean that the traditional system of three invariable psalms at Compline will be restored; these are psalms 4, 90, and 133, given only for Sunday Compline in the Roman office; considered as night prayers they are admirably chosen for this hour.

The hour of Matins presents a special problem. Liturgically, it is of monastic origin (4th century), but the idea behind it can be traced back to the very ancient practice of prayer at midnight. A very rich symbolism was attached to this hour: it was bound up with the idea of the Parousia, and had the character of a vigil in preparation for Christ's return; for he promised that he would return "like a thief in the night." When celebrated in choir Matins will retain its character of nocturnal praise (*nocturna laus*); but it will be so adapted that it may be recited at any hour of the day. Provision is, therefore, made for those who are incapable of observing the traditional hour for this prayer. The adaptation will obviously consist in a new selection of hymns, so that a priest saying his office in the afternoon will not be obliged to intone *"Nox atra rerum contegit . . ."* ("Dark night has covered all the colors of the earth.")

"The hour of Prime is to be suppressed." This ruling is by no means arbitrary: the aim is to restore a balance to the morning office, which has become overcrowded. Lauds, as we have seen, is *the* morning office. Prime, on the other hand, a prayer of purely monastic origin, is simply a duplication of Lauds; it is the only hour to disappear.

"In choir the hours of Terce, Sext, and None are to be observed. But outside choir it will be lawful to select any one of these three, according to the time of day." It is noteworthy that the Council seems to attach more importance to the principle of proper correspondence between the time of the day and its appropriate hour than to the mere volume of liturgical prayer. Certainly, this is a considerable concession to all engaged in the active ministry and will go far to lighten the daily burden of the office. The liturgical hours should now come to be regarded not so much as the *onus diei* (the daily burden) as the *opus dei* (the work of God) which was how St. Benedict termed the divine office.

The maternal solicitude of the Church prompts her, in certain circumstances, to authorize total dispensations from the obligation of the office: "In particular cases, and for adequate reasons, ordinaries can dispense their subjects wholly or in part from the obligation of reciting the divine office, or they can commute the obligation" (Art. 97). The term *ordinary* must be understood according to the definition of canon 198 of the Code of Canon Law: the term includes not only the bishop but, also, the major superiors of exempt clerical religious orders for their subjects.

THE CONTENT OF THE NEW OFFICE

What will the office of the near future be like,

and how will it differ from the existing one? The answer to our query is given in broad outline in Arts. 91-93.

The psalms will continue to form the substance of our prayer. But the principle whereby all 150 psalms were recited in the course of a week has not been maintained. Henceforth "the psalms are no longer to be distributed throughout one week, but through some longer period of time" (Art. 91). What this period will be remains to be seen; some suggest a biweekly period, as is the custom in the Milanese rite, but it could be extended to a tri-weekly or even a monthly cycle.

Matins will be made up of fewer psalms and longer reading (Art. 89). There will be a new version of the psalms: "The work of revising the psalter, already happily begun, is to be finished as soon as possible. . . ." This announcement may surprise some readers: what of the Latin version of the psalter published in 1945 by the Pontifical Biblical Institute? It is now recognized that this version, although a scholarly work, is far from sat-isfactory from a liturgical point of view, being unsuited to choral celebration. The language, al-though carefully constructed and polished from a classicist's point of view, represents too great a cleavage with traditional Christian Latin: it is the Latin of Cicero rather than that of the great West-ern Fathers. The psalter of the future will be closer to that of St. Jerome, the one with which we are most familiar, but this ancient version will be thor-oughly revised in the light of modern scholarship.[2]

[2] It is known that Pope John XXIII thought highly of a recent revision of the Latin psalter executed at the request of the Benedictine General Synod of Abbots: *Psalterii Nova Recensio;* cura et studio R. Weber, m.b. Abbaye S. Maurice et S. Maur, Clervaux, 1961.

The Constitution attaches great importance to the readings of the office. A special place of honor will be given to the reading of sacred Scripture, for the Church realizes that the word of God is never so efficacious as when read in a liturgical context. (For a full statement of principle concerning the reading of sacred Scripture in the liturgy, *cf.* Ch. 1, Art. 24; also Ch. 2, Art. 51.) There will be longer and better-chosen lessons from the Old and New Testaments.

The same principle with regard to length and variety will hold for the patristic lessons. The repertoire of patristic sermons contained in the Roman Breviary is a rather limited one. Very often the message we manage to extract from a particular lesson has little immediacy or relevance for modern minds. It should be pointed out, however, that to judge these lessons fairly it is necessary to read them in their original context; in other words, it is necessary to read the full sermon as published in the various collections of the Fathers. Originally the full sermon was read in the course of the office; at the end of the medieval period, however, the lessons were drastically shortened with little regard for content or context, with the result that what has survived consists, in many instances, of mere snippets or token readings.[3]

It is to be hoped that the Eastern Fathers will be better represented—one would like, for example, to see included some of the catechetical sermons of St. Cyril of Jerusalem. The Constitution includes among its "authors" (*auctores*), "the fathers, doctors and other ecclesiastical writers." It seems rea-

[3] For an excellent treatment of the lessons of the Breviary, cf. *L'Office Divine,* by Dom Pierre Salmon (Editions du Cerf, 1959): ch. IV, *Les lectures de l'office.*

sonable to presume that this latter term is wide
enough to include some of the great spiritual
writers of modern times. (One could, for instance,
visualize a sermon by Cardinal Newman being
completely at home in such a collection.) The accounts of the lives of the saints will be rewritten
so as to make them "accord with the facts of history" (Art. 92).

The hymns of the Breviary are to be revised, or
rather restored. Art. 93 decrees: "To whatever extent may seem desirable, the hymns are to be
restored to their original form . . . Also, as occasion
may arise, let other selections from the treasury of
hymns be incorporated into the divine office." Here
is a long-awaited reform. It was in the seventeenth
century by order of Pope Urban VIII that the
liturgical hymns were radically revised with a view
to making them conform to classical standards of
style, expression and meter. The result was a serious
impoverishment of these ancient hymns, charac-
terized, above all, by their simple, rugged beauty,
and their spontaneous, virile piety. The original
versions of the hymns, which have been retained
in the monastic office, will now be incorporated
into the Roman Breviary.

COMMUNAL CELEBRATION

Art. 95 decrees that "Communities obliged to
choral office are bound to celebrate the office in
choir every day in addition to their conventual
Mass." (The communities affected by this law are
then listed.)

"Clerics not bound to office in choir, if they are
in major orders, are bound to pray the entire office
every day, either in common or privately . . ."
(Art. 96).

"The occasions on which parts of the office may be replaced by liturgical services are to be defined by the rubrics" (Art. 97). This is an extension of the concession contained in the Code of Rubrics of 1960 (n. 85) with regard to the recitation of the Greater Litanies.[4]

As stated above, the Constitution attaches the greatest importance to the celebration of the office in common. The doctrine of the Mystical Body is the underlying reason for this preference. ". . . priests who live together, or assemble for any purpose, are urged to pray at least some part of the divine office in common" (Art. 99). We may conclude from this insistence on the public character of the divine office that the choral structure of the Breviary, made up of the responsories, antiphons, versicles, etc. will be retained: the Breviary, being the Prayer Book of the Church could never be made to resemble a book of private devotions.

A further stimulus to choral celebration is the rather momentous concession conferred in Art. 96, which particularly affects nuns and others not bound to the divine office: "Religious who, according to their constitutions, are to recite parts of the divine office, are thereby joining in the public prayer of the Church. The same may be said of those who, in virtue of their constitutions, recite any short office, provided this be drawn up after the pattern of the divine office and has been duly approved."

This concession will be received with joy and gratitude by great numbers of religious. These

[4] Cf. "The Pastoral Significance of the New Code of Rubrics" by Rev. P. Muldoon; published in *Studies in Pastoral Liturgy II* (Ed. V. Ryan, o.s.b.; The Furrow Trust—Gill and Son, Dublin, 1963); cf. p. 206.

short forms of the office which hitherto would have
fallen under the definition of *pia exercitia* ("Devotions"), have now been raised to the status of liturgical prayers, with all the prerogatives which
that prayer possesses. To understand the difference
between liturgical and non-liturgical prayers and
actions, the reader would do well to consult the
definition given in the 1958 Instruction on *Sacred
Music and Liturgy* (Art. 1, Ch. 1). The Instruction
states that "those sacred actions are 'liturgical'
which from the institution of Jesus Christ or the
Church and in their name, are carried out in accordance with the liturgical books approved by the
Holy See, by persons legitimately deputed. . . ."
This mandate to represent the Church officially in
its public prayer is now given to all religious. These
simple forms of the Breviary will now be included
among the Church's liturgical books.[5]

The laity, too, are to be drawn more and more
into the Church's official worship; the faithful must
also lend their voices to the homage of praise which
the Church daily offers to God. Pope Pius XII's
desire to see the public celebration of Vespers restored to parish churches as part of the Sunday
worship should now be fully realized. Art. 100 lays
down: "Parish priests should see to it that the chief
hours, especially Vespers, are celebrated in common
in the Church on Sundays and the more solemn
feasts." By "chief hours" (*horae praecipuae*) is
meant the hours of Lauds and Vespers, according
to the definition given in Art. 89 (a). As we shall
see in our treatment of Art. 101 of this chapter,

[5] The best commentary on the article of the Instruction
quoted above is that given in *Liturgie et Musique,* by
A. G. Martimort et F. Picard (Editions du Cerf 1959); *cf.*
pp. 21-25.

the use of the vernacular will be permitted at the public celebration of these hours.

THE VERNACULAR

As a general principle it can be stated that priests and lesser clerics will continue to pray the office in Latin, whereas almost unrestricted use of the vernacular is granted to religious who are not clerics.

The whole question of the vernacular is dealt with succinctly in Art. 101. It may come as a disappointment to many priests that this latitude with regard to the language of the office has not been extended to them as well. The Constitution, however, makes the following generous provision: "But in individual cases the ordinary has power to grant the use of the vernacular to those clerics for whom Latin constitutes a grave obstacle to their praying the office as it should be prayed." The grave obstacle (*grave impedimentum*) could consist in a defective knowledge of Latin or even, perhaps, in a genuine psychological difficulty in praying in that language. Again, it should be noted, as in Art. 97, that the term *ordinary* includes the major superiors of exempt clerical religious orders.

Since the adoption of the vernacular is a great aid toward conscious participation in the liturgy, the Constitution makes the following concession to non-clerics: "The competent superior (*Superior competens*) has the power to concede the use of the vernacular for the divine office, even in choir, to religious, including men who are not clerics. The version, however, must be one that is approved" (101 §3). It would seem that the term *Superior competens* designates the major superior (and thus, normally, the Provincial), but this is not perfectly clear from the context.

An interesting question arises out of Art. 100 concerning the public celebration of Lauds and Vespers in parish churches. May these major hours be celebrated in the vernacular? The Constitution does not explicitly say so, but this can certainly be inferred from the general principles relative to the vernacular given in the first two chapters of the Constitution (Ch. 1, Arts. 21, 27, 30, 36 §2; Ch. 2, Art. 54). Art. 100 encourages the faithful to pray the divine office with their priests, or among themselves or even individually, and this presumably in the vernacular. Moreover, we learn from the final paragraph of Art. 101 that the priest who prays the office in the vernacular with a group of the faithful, or with religious, is fulfilling his obligation to the divine office.

Discussion Questions

1. On what fact is the superiority of choral, or common, celebration over solitary celebration of the office based?
2. How has the revision of the office resulted in a more practical horarium?
3. What are the "two hinges on which the daily office turns"?
4. What hour of the office is simply a duplication of Lauds?
5. What is the difference between liturgical and non-liturgical prayers and actions?
6. To what extent is the content of the office to be revised?
7. Why should the laity lend their voices to the homage of praise which the Church daily offers to God in the divine office?
8. Who may, or may not, pray the office in the vernacular?

My Apostolate

1. No amount of apostolic work will bear much fruit unless it is sustained by a life of prayer, and no prayer is more efficacious than that spoken by the Church in her sacred liturgy. Consequently, I shall try to read at least one hour of the divine office every day.
2. In order that the divine office shall become a personal, conscious, and deeply interior prayer, I shall try to acquire an understanding of, and relish for, the psalms. A commentary on the psalms will help me in this matter.

5 The Liturgical Year

Vincent Ryan, O.S.B.

T HE chief interest of this chapter lies in its doctrine. It presents us with a splendid theological vision of the liturgical year in which everything is centered on Christ and on his redeeming work. Comparing this chapter with the relevant sections of *Mediator Dei,* we perceive a continuity of thought but also a distinct doctrinal development. By introducing the concepts of the *mystery of Christ* and the *paschal mystery* it completes the teaching of Pope Pius XII and offers a more unified and Christocentric approach to the liturgical year.

THE MYSTERY OF CHRIST

The terms *mystery of Christ* and *paschal mystery* represent key concepts in the Constitution. We are constantly meeting these terms, especially the second of them, not only in this chapter but throughout the entire document, viz., in the introductory chapter (Arts. 2, 5, 6, 10, 16), with reference to the eucharist (Art. 47), and to the sacraments and sacramentals (Arts. 61, 81). The Council has thus brought to fruition the speculation of biblicists and theologians who in recent years have been in-

creasingly pre-occupied with the ideas which un-
derlie these terms.

What is the mystery of Christ? The expression is
at first a little bewildering, but a meditative reading of the passages in St. Paul where the word
occurs will bring its meaning into focus.[1] Basically
the mystery is no other than Christ himself considered as the fulfillment of God's eternal plan to
save the human race—a plan which is realized in
successive stages covering the whole range of human
history. The Pauline notion of the mystery of
Christ is well summarized by Dom Cyprian Vagaggini in his famous study, *The Theological Dimensions of the Liturgy*[2] in the following passage:

> We are therefore remaining faithful to the
> thinking of St. Paul if we use the expression
> "mystery of Christ" to refer to everything that
> the incarnate Word, Savior and High Priest of
> the human race, is and does in the divine plan
> and its realization. We can equivalate "history
> of salvation," "mystery," "mystery of Christ":
> the concern is always with a single reality, in-
> asmuch as the center of this sacred history, this
> mystery, is Christ.

These considerations will enable us to understand
the function and scope of the liturgical year so
clearly enunciated in Art. 101:

> As each year passes by, she (the Church) unfolds
> the whole mystery of Christ, from the incarna-
> tion and birth until the ascension, the day of
> Pentecost and the expectation of blessed hope
> and of the coming of the Lord.

[1] The most pregnant text is Ephesians 3, 1-13; cf. also, Rom.
16, 25; 1 Cor. 2, 7; Eph. 3, 9 and 5, 32; Col. 1, 26.

[2] Vol. I published by the Liturgical Press, Collegeville, Min-
nesota, 1959. Cf. p. 9.

But it was essentially by his paschal mystery that Christ reconciled the world to his Father. In this mystery the passion, death and resurrection of Our Lord form three aspects of a single reality, that of man's redemption.[3] Father Dalmais, in a recent work, has given us this useful and comprehensive definition of the paschal mystery[4]:

> The paschal mystery is the fulfillment of God's great plan for the reconciliation of mankind to himself in Christ and for the summoning of men to share in heavenly benefits by causing to dwell in them the Holy Ghost who initiates them into the divine life.

Immediately we see the importance of the Temporal cycle wholly centered on the saving mysteries of Christ, of which the annual commemoration of the paschal mystery is the summit and crown, and Sunday, the Lord's day, its weekly re-enactment. Easter is not only the heart of the liturgical year, it is also the radiant center which sheds its light on all the Church's seasons and feasts.

We are now in a better position to appreciate the wisdom of the 1960 Code of Rubrics which had secured the pre-eminence of the Temporal cycle. In Arts. 108 and 111 of the Constitution this primacy of the feasts of Our Lord is re-affirmed:

Therefore the proper of the time must be given the preference which is its due over the feasts of the saints, so that the entire cycle of the mysteries of salvation may be suitably recalled.

---

[3] Cf. . A. Jungmann, s.j.: "The History of Holy Week as the Heart of the Liturgical Year." Article published in *Studies in Pastoral Liturgy*, vol. I. (Edited by Placid Murray, o.s.b. The Furrow Trust, Maynooth, 1961).

[4] *Introduction to the Liturgy*, published by G. Chapman, London, 1961. Cf. p. 78.

PREPARING FOR THE PASCH

To ensure a more fruitful participation of the faithful in the annual celebration of the paschal mystery, the Council has, in Arts. 109 and 110, established the principles for a renewal of the Lenten liturgy:

> The season of Lent has a twofold character; primarily by recalling or preparing for baptism and penance, it disposes the faithful who persevere in hearing the word of God and in prayer, to celebrate the paschal mystery. This twofold character is to be brought into greater prominence both in the liturgy and by instruction.

How will the baptismal character of Lent be brought into greater prominence? One method will be to exploit to better advantage the rich baptismal catechesis contained in the Scripture readings. The Lenten Mass formularies have preserved some of the great traditional gospel texts which were once made use of to instruct the catechumens on the mystery of baptism. Unfortunately there has been a displacement. With the disappearance of adult baptism in Rome (6th-7th centuries), these gospels which were originally read on the third, fourth and fifth Sundays of Lent, were relegated to weekdays. The gospels in question are those which are now read on the Friday of the third week of Lent, the Wednesday of the fourth week, and the Friday of the fifth week; they treat of Christ's discourse to the Samaritan woman (John 4, 5-42), the healing of the blind man at the pool of Siloe (John 9, 1-38) and the raising of Lazarus (John 11, 1-45).

These great gospel pericopes which contain a mine of teaching on the mystery of baptism will probably be restored to their appropriate Sundays;

in this way greater numbers of the faithful will be enabled to profit by them and so be disposed to renew their baptismal vows on Easter night. The Old Testament readings which accompany these gospels in our missals will also be restored to the Sunday liturgy; in them the sacrament of cleansing and rebirth is admirably prefigured.

We learn from Art. 69 of Ch. 3 (The Sacraments and Sacramentals) that the catechumenate for adults is to be restored, and is to comprise several distinct steps each of which is to be sanctified by sacred rites. It would be very fitting if at least some of these sacred rites were conferred during the Sundays of Lent, thus bringing into greater prominence the baptismal character of this season. This would be a return to the ancient Roman discipline of the catechumenate when, in the course of Lent, the candidates for baptism received the various preparatory rites, known as the "scrutinies." The public nature of these ceremonies, each accompanied by a special Mass offered for the catechumens, was a great incentive for the Christian community to pray for these *electi* whom they would soon be welcoming as brethren and fully-fledged members of the Church.

The penitential features of Lent are also to be given greater prominence, with special emphasis on the social aspect of penance: "During Lent penance should not only be internal and individual but also external and social."

The doctrine of the Mystical Body underlies this insistence on the social nature of penance. The Church is not made up of private individuals but of members of a body. Just as the meritorious actions of individual Christians rebound to the good of the entire body, so sin inflicts an injury on the entire Church.

There is no question here of restoring the ancient discipline of public penance, but the Church has much to gain by borrowing something of its spirit. The ceremony of the imposition of ashes at the beginning of Lent, for example, is an excellent corporate manifestation of guilt and penance. Other elements in the Lenten liturgy, e.g. the Scripture readings, could be exploited to foster among the faithful a deeper awareness of the social consequences of sin. Some public ceremony corresponding to the rite of reconciliation of penitents, which once formed part of the Holy Thursday liturgy, could also be restored.

The Constitution stresses the role of the Church in the reconciliation of penitents: "the role of the Church in penitential practices (*partes ecclesiae in actione paenitentiali*) is not to be passed over, and the people must be exhorted to pray for sinners." This is a significant phrase and merits close attention; it should help to counteract the tendency to view the sacrament of penance in too individualistic a light. A citation from Schillebeeckx's *Christ the Sacrament*[5] will form a suitable commentary on this text:

> The ecclesial effect of the sacrament of penance is reconciliation with the Church as the sacrament of our reconciliation with God in Christ. The Church is the earthly manifestation of God's redeeming mercy, and Confession is visible contact with the Church precisely under this aspect. It establishes us in the ecclesial status of penitents who, by the performance of the penance required by the Church and through the mercy

5 Published by Sheed and Ward, 1963. Cf. p. 217.

of her absolution, become reconciled with God himself.

THE WEEKLY PASCH

The description of Sunday as "the weekly Easter," has become a little hackneyed; but while we are familiar with the phrase itself, we are probably far from realizing its full implications. A careful reading of Art. 106 which treats of the Lord's day will leave one in no doubt as to the inestimable importance of Sunday in the mind of the Church. The opening words of this article have the ring of a solemn proclamation:

> By a tradition handed down from the apostles and going back to the very day of Christ's resurrection, the Church celebrates the paschal mystery every eighth day. . . .

The Constitution then goes on to describe in what this weekly celebration of the pasch consists:

> For on this day Christ's faithful should come together into one place so that, by hearing the word of God and taking part in the eucharist, they may call to mind the passion, resurrection and glorification of the Lord Jesus, and may thank God who "has begotten them again, through the resurrection of Jesus Christ from the dead, unto a living hope" (1 Pet. 1, 3).

With that concision so characteristic of the Constitution, we have in this brief paragraph a veritable theology of the Lord's day—a theology of great depth and richness. Sunday is shown to be the day *par excellence* of the Christian assembly, when the faithful gather together in one place to hear the word of God and to offer the Holy Sacrifice.[6] In

---

[6] Cf. Charles Davis: "The Mass as the Assembly of Christians" in *Studies in Pastoral Liturgy*, vol. II (Edited by V. Ryan, O.S.B. Published by the Furrow Trust—Gill, 1963).

the sacrifice of the Mass the Church brings to mind the entire saving work of Christ, "his passion, resurrection and glorification." In the celebration of the eucharist the mystery of redemption is sacramentally renewed. To quote again from Vagaggini:

> Every Mass expresses synthetically and realizes in its own way the whole mystery of Christ.[7]

The paschal mystery is then, in a very special way, renewed each week. That is why the Constitution declares that this day should be one of joy and of freedom from work. It is in the sacramental renewal of the paschal mystery that the People of God give thanks to God "for his unspeakable gift" (2 Cor. 9, 15)—the gift of redemption.

A splendid unity is seen to exist between the two parts of the Mass, viz., the liturgy of the word and the eucharistic sacrifice. It is in hearing God's wonderful deeds, the *mirabilia Dei,* proclaimed in the service of the word, that the faithful are disposed to take their part in the offering of the Mass itself.

It follows from these considerations that the Lord's day must enjoy a place of pre-eminence in the Christian calendar. The Council has conceded to it a dignity that is only surpassed by that of Easter itself: "Hence the Lord's day is the original feast day *(primordialis dies festus)* . . . Other celebrations, unless they be truly of great importance, must not have precedence over the Sunday which is the *foundation and kernel of the whole liturgical year"* (italics my own).

The Saints

The Constitution in assigning to the sanctoral cycle a subordinate place in the liturgical year, in no way derogates from the cult of the saints. The

[7] Op. cit., p. 75.

Liturgical seasons and the feasts of Our Lord must be given precedence, but, fundamentally, there is no opposition between the temporal and sanctoral cycles in the Christian calendar.

The Constitution, in stressing the Christological aspect of the sanctoral cycle, brings to light the underlying unity that exists between the two cycles. The saints by their lives echo the cry of St. Paul, "I live, now not I, but Christ liveth in me" (Gal. 2, 20). In the saints Christ relives his paschal mystery. We are here reminded of the theme, so dear to St. Cyprian and the early Fathers, of Christ victorious in his martyrs: "and he who overcame death for us, ever overcomes it in us."[8]

It is not only the martyrs, but the *confessores,* too, who manifest the paschal mystery in their lives. They share Christ's victory over sin and death not by laying down their lives but by the perfection of their faith and witness: "this is the victory that triumphs over the world, our faith" (1 John 5, 4).

Sanctity is but the full blossoming of the grace received at baptism by which we are drawn into the mystery of Christ's death and resurrection. Thus, in the opening chapter of the Constitution (Art. 6), we are told that "by baptism men are plunged into the paschal mystery of Christ; they die with him, are buried with him and rise with him. . . ."

Christian perfection is the realization on the moral plane of the mystery inaugurated at baptism. As Abbot Marmion so well expressed it in *Christ the Life of the Soul:*[9]

Christian life is nothing else but the progressive and continuous development, the practical ap-

8 Epistle X.
9 Part 2, section 2 ("Death and Life").

plication throughout our whole life, of this
double supernatural result of "death" and of
"life" produced by baptism.

Perhaps these considerations will help us to grasp
the force and import of expressions such as: "By
celebrating the passage of these saints from earth
to heaven the Church proclaims the paschal mystery achieved in those who have suffered and been
glorified with Christ" (Art. 104).

The Constitution thus guards us against an exag-
gerated cult of the saints and from the tendency to
view them as isolated individuals unrelated to the
mystery of Christ. In the liturgy the Church contemplates Christ in his saints. The endless variety of
sanctity which they display and which is the effect of
the multiform grace of God, reflects something of
the infinite riches of Christ. This is an added reason
for our honoring the saints and is clearly indicated
in Art. 111: "For the feasts of the saints proclaim
the wonderful works of Christ in his servants, and
display to the faithful fitting examples for their
imitation."

The privileged place which Our Lady has always
held in the Church's cycle of feasts is solemnly re-
affirmed in Art. 103, but again in the context of the
mystery of her divine Son.

In celebrating this annual cycle of Christ's mysteries, Holy Church honors with special love the
Blessed Mary, Mother of God, who is insepara-
bly involved in the saving work of her Son. In
her the Church holds up and admires the most
perfect fruit of the redemption . . .

APPENDIX: REVISION OF CALENDAR

A declaration of the Council on the revision of the
Calendar is added as an appendix to Ch. 5. An interesting account of the debate on this subject and that

of a fixed Easter is given by Father Antoine Wenger in his book *Vatican II: Première Sesson*.[10]

Concern was expressed by many of the Fathers at the divorce between the civil and liturgical calendars. "The Church would like to avoid this hiatus in order to continue, as in ages past, to impregnate the rhythm of time with the Christian spirit which has its source in the paschal cycle."

It seems that Cardinal Feltin was the leading advocate of this reform. He strongly urged the stablishment of a fixed date for the celebration of Easter. The reasons which he adduced were mainly pastoral: such a reform would greatly facilitate the pastoral life of parishes as well as the organization of dioceses. He also remarked that in France, as well as in other countries, school and university holidays were no longer made to coincide with the actual date of Easter. The result of this divergence was a notable depreciation of Easter in civil life as well as a falling off of attendance at the Holy Week ceremonies.

In consideration of these and similar views the Constitution declares that "The sacred Council would not object if the feast of Easter were assigned to a particular Sunday of the Gregorian Calendar, provided that others whom it may concern, especially the brethren who are not in communion with the Holy See, are agreed on this matter."

The proviso with regard to the separated brethren introduces a delicate ecumenical note. The Eastern Churches did not follow Rome's example when, under Pope Gregory XIII, it decided on a reform of the Julian Calendar. Today a double calendar is in use in the Greek Churches: the Julian Calendar

[10] Published by Editions du Centurion, Paris, 1963 (Series, L'Eglise en son Temps); cf. pp. 94 ff.

is followed for the paschal cycle, the Gregorian Calendar for the fixed feasts. In the Russian Church only the Julian Calendar is employed.

Although the fixation of Easter would represent a departure from tradition, the scholars seem to be agreed that there is here no liturgical principle at stake. An authority on the Christian calendar, Mme Noële Denis-Boulet, sees no reason "why it (the Christian religion) should be tied indefinitely to a luni-solar calendar . . . whose grave imperfections were felt by liturgists long before modern States worried about them."[11]

As to the actual date to be assigned to Easter, this author suggests the first Sunday after April 7 (the date on which, according to most exegetes, Jesus underwent his passion in the year 30) .

11 *The Christian Calendar;* a Faith and Fact Book (London: Burns and Oates, 1960); cf. pp. 108 ff.

Discussion Questions

1. What does the term *mystery of Christ* mean?
2. What does the term *paschal mystery* mean?
3. What is the summit and crown of the liturgical year?
4. What is the twofold character of the season of Lent?
5. In what does the weekly celebration of the pasch consist?
6. What is the foundation and kernel of the whole liturgical year?
7. At present, is there any opposition between the temporal and sanctoral cycles in the Christian calendar?
8. What is the Christian life?
9. What do you think about assigning the feast of Easter to a particular Sunday of the Gregorian calendar?

My Apostolate

1. The doctrine of the Mystical Body underlies the Church's insistence on the social nature of penance. The Church is not made up of private individuals but of members of a body. Just as the meritorious actions of individual Christians rebound to the good of the entire body, so sin inflicts an injury on the entire Church. An appreciation of this truth will deepen my awareness of the social consequences of sin.

2. In the liturgy the Church contemplates Christ in his saints. The endless variety of sanctity which the saints display, and which is the effect of the multiform grace of God, reflects the infinite riches of Christ. This is an added reason for devotion to at least my patron saint.

6 Sacred Music

Kieran O'Gorman

ARTICLE 113 of the brief but eloquent chapter on Sacred Music states:

Liturgical worship is given a more noble form when the divine offices are celebrated solemnly in song, with the assistance of sacred ministers and the active participation of the people.

The musical tradition of the Church is very highly valued by the Council which places it above any other art, because it forms "a necessary or integral part of the solemn liturgy." This high place has been earned especially by Gregorian Chant which, in a sense grew up with the liturgy and is still to be given pride of place in liturgical functions (Art. 116). But Gregorian Chant is wedded to the Latin language and this is a union which no man should put asunder.

What then will happen now that it is possible that the vernacular may be used in parts of the Mass? (Those who may want to sing the Office in the vernacular will be very few.) This question raises many problems the solution to which can only be guessed at until more directives have come and our hierarchy have decided what parts of the Mass, if any, will be sung in the vernacular. Yet it may not be out of place to examine some of these problems.

The Constitution recommends that in those Masses, which are celebrated with the people, a suitable place may be allotted to their mother-tongue. "This is to apply in the first place to the readings and Prayer of the Faithful, but also as local conditions may warrant, to those items of the liturgy which pertain to the people . . . Nevertheless steps must be taken to insure that the faithful are able to say or to sing together also in Latin, those parts of the Ordinary of the Mass which are rightfully theirs" (Art. 54). This seems to say that while they may sing pieces in the vernacular (if the bishops permit it or think it wise) the people must also know these chants in Latin. I can see very little need for discarding the Greek phrases *Kyrie eleison, Christe eleison*. These were retained when the Roman Church began to use Latin instead of Greek and are easily learned and understood. Besides, they have the advantage of good musical settings. There are eighteen settings, not counting the "adlibitum" chants, in the Graduale and though most of these are too elaborate and too outmodish (if I may give the word a slight twist) for good congregational singing, they are but a fraction of some 200 settings. Many of these may be made available in the new editions of liturgical songbooks which are to be completed, or in the edition to be brought out containing simpler chants for use in small churches (Art. 117).

Incidentally, this directive to provide books for smaller churches and the appeal to composers to provide also for the needs of small choirs and for the active participation of the entire assembly of the faithful (Art. 121) shows a very welcome pas-

toral note missing in previous pronouncements on
sacred music.

If a modern setting of the *Kyrie* is to be selected
it should be one which is agreed on not only
throughout Ireland but also England, Scotland,
Wales and if possible America.

The *Gloria* and the Creed are both rather long
chants which the ordinary congregation should not
be expected to pray-sing in Latin. Indeed many of
those now singing them know little beyond the
facts that the *Gloria* is a hymn of praise and the
Credo a profession of faith. But how can they praise
when they do not know the words they are using,
how can they make an act of faith when they do
not know just what it is in which they are profess-
ing belief? It would seem desirable that these
chants, at least, should be in the mother-tongue.
There is some speculation that the Nicean Creed
may be replaced by the Apostles' Creed, while in
Holland they are urging that in its place we should
sing a "gospel song" based on the gospel of the day.

The same can hardly be said of the *Sanctus*. This
is a rather short chant containing but some twenty
words easily understood. If the Preface is to remain
in Latin and if, as is likely, the celebrant will sing
the *Sanctus* with the congregation before beginning the *Te Igitur,* then it would be a pity to break
into another language, and perhaps into another
melody, when the simple, noble melody of *Sanctus
XVIII* flows naturally out of the melody of the
Preface.

The *Agnus Dei* is, in a very real sense, out on its
own. It does not flow from the action of the Mass
but was introduced to occupy the congregation during the "breaking of the bread" (a rather long

ceremony in the early Church). It makes a fine preparation for Holy Communion.

The choir has two types of chant to sing at a High Mass or *Missa Cantata*. One is the processional chant—Introit, Offertory and Communion; the other is the responsorial—Gradual, Tract and/ or Alleluia. This latter type, known as the *canto di riposo* in Italian, was the musical highlight of the Mass and gave its name to the book containing the chants of the Mass, the "Graduale." Since then the musical emphasis has shifted to the parts of the Mass belonging to the congregation. Now, that the aim of the restoration of the liturgy is clearly stated to be the active participation by the people, we may expect that the processional chants will be adapted in such a way that the people will join in them by repeating a refrain—in the same way as the "Gelineau" psalms are sung—and the choir's main function, apart from leading and assisting all the singing, will be to cloak the moment of meditative silence after the reading of the first Scripture lesson with an aura of prayer.

Finally, there are the chants of the sacred ministers. If the Epistle and Gospel are to be chanted in the vernacular, a suitable recitatif must be found. At present, a group of church musicians are working on this problem, trying to find a recitatif which would suit many languages. The difficulty is that each language has its own peculiar cadences and it is at these that the musical inflections are made.

These are some of the speculations to which the Constitution gives rise.

A few other points may be worth noting. According to Art. 50 "elements in the Mass which came to be duplicated are to be discarded." This will mean that the celebrant no longer will have to read the Introit, Gradual, Tract, Alleluia, Sequence, Offertory or Communion since these will be sung by the choir and people, or the *Kyrie, Gloria, Credo, Sanctus and Agnus Dei.* Each person will "do all of, but only, those parts which pertain to his office . . ." (Art. 28). This may lead to a marked difference between what is read at a Low Mass and at a High Mass. The pipe organ is to be given preference in the church, but other instruments may be admitted with the knowledge and consent of the competent territorial authorities.

Stress is again laid on the teaching and practice of music in all religious houses and seminaries. This means there must be competent musical teachers and in this context it is lamentable the little use that has been made of the Pontifical Institute of Sacred Music in Rome.

It is good to read the recommendation that a more critical edition of books of sacred music is to be published. In fact, the critical editions of the Kyriale and Graduale are almost ready.

It is likely that as new church music will be needed, composers will be encouraged to turn their minds to other pieces rather than those of the Common of the Mass. They should be protected by the laws of copyright and the large-scale copying which now exists should be discouraged.

There will be large-scale changes which may take many decades before they are finalized. The aim remains as that stated by St. Pius X sixty years ago, that the people must take an active part in the liturgy. We cannot boast that we have listened in the past. When the competent ecclesiastical authorities set up a liturgical commission to regulate pastoral liturgical action throughout the territory, let each resolve to cooperate as best he can so that full use may be made of the liturgy as "the outstanding means whereby the faithful may express in their lives and manifest to others, the mystery of Christ and the real nature of the true Church" (Art. 2).

Discussion Questions

1. Why is the musical tradition of the Church very highly valued by the Council?
2. In those Masses which are celebrated with the people, where does the Constitution recommend the use of the vernacular?
3. Would you want to sing the divine office in the vernacular?
4. What does Art. 54 have to say about the vernacular in the Mass?
5. What are the two main types of chant at a High Mass?
6. What is a "recitatif"?
7. What does the term "cadence" mean?
8. What does Art. 121 have to say about composers of sacred music?

My Apostolate

1. Because the musical tradition of the Church forms a necessary or integral part of the solemn liturgy, I shall participate actively *in song* at those solemn celebrations whenever possible.
2. Since Gregorian Chant "is still to be given pride of place in liturgical functions," it would not be such a bad idea for me to grasp the basic principles behind this ritual plain song of the Church. A trip to my neighborhood library would be a good start toward this goal.

7 Sacred Art

Donal O'Sullivan, S.J.

CHAPTER seven of the Constitution on the Sacred Liturgy, *Of Sacred Arts and Furnishings,* must be read in the light of the preceding chapters. These chapters make repeated references to the paschal mystery and to the insertion of the Christian into it by his participation in the liturgy. It is a re-formed liturgy; and this final chapter of the Constitution indicates that a re-formed art is to go hand in hand, or rather, soul in soul with it. In this respect Art. 107 of Ch. 5 would seem to be of capital importance. "The liturgical year is to be revised so that the traditional customs and training methods of the sacred seasons shall be preserved, or else restored to suit the condition of modern times; their specific character is to be retained, so that they duly nourish the piety of the faithful who celebrate the mysteries of Christian redemption, especially the paschal mystery." The same emphasis, though this time from a more legal aspect, is perceptible in Art. 128. It deals with laws on art, architecture and furnishings. "Any laws which seem less suited to the reformed liturgy are to be brought into harmony with it, or else abrogated."

The opening sentences of this chapter on the arts plead, like Gerard Manley Hopkins, that beauty be given back to God, "beauty's self and beauty's giver." "All things set apart for use in divine worship should be truly worthy, becoming and beautiful." The Church reserves to herself the right to judge what is "fitted for sacred use." But she "has admitted changes in materials, style or ornamentation prompted by the progress of the technical arts with the passage of time."

Art. 123 should settle the perhaps over-acrimonious disputes of recent years as to the existence of an ecclesiastical "style." "The Church has not adopted any particular style of art as her very own; she has admitted styles from every period according to the natural dispositions and circumstances of her peoples, and the needs of the various rites. Thus, in the course of the centuries, she has amassed a treasury of art which must be very carefully preserved. The art of our own days, coming from every race and region, is also to be given free scope provided that it adorns the sacred buildings and holy rites with due reverence and honor; thereby it is enabled to contribute its own voice to that wonderful chorus of praise in honor of the Catholic faith sung by great men in times gone by."

After the Council, then, there can be no question as to the right of contemporary art to praise God and edify his children, provided it brings "due reverence and honor" to its elevated task. "Noble beauty" not "sumptuous display" is laid down as the norm for bishops in their choice of "a truly sacred art." They are "carefully and insistently" to remove works "which do not accord with faith, morals and Christian piety and which offend true religious sense either by depraved forms or by lack of artistic worth, mediocrity and pretense" (Art. 124). The Council has previously described in the Constitution the ideal of Christian piety—it differs from the popular acceptance of the word—and one of its main tasks has been precisely to recall us to a *true* religious sense as opposed to an empty and false traditionalism. Following Pope John, it is substituting genuine tradition for fossilized conventions. Many of the laity, many priests too, have become attached to those conventions; and one must not underestimate the imaginative shock they are bound to experience when the "depraved forms" of the commercialized Hollywood-type "art" are taken from them. "Lack of artistic worth, mediocrity and pretense" is only too terribly descriptive of the content of many churches. Bishops are indeed worthy of sympathy, not criticism, in the herculean task which has been imposed upon them by this one paragraph of the Constitution.

Not that the Council has fallen, after the lapse of centuries, into a new iconoclastic heresy! "The practice of placing statues and pictures in churches so that they may be venerated by the faithful is to be maintained; but their number should be moderate and their relative positions should exemplify right order." And why the importance of this right order? "For otherwise they might corrupt the people's sense of values and foster devotions of doubtful orthodoxy" (Art. 125). It is that "sense of values," that Pope John and his Council have restored to the *plebs sancta Dei.*

And what of the Church's churches? A wise brevity is here the soul of her architectural brief. "And when churches are to be built, ordinaries must see to it that the design of these churches is such as to facilitate the celebration of the liturgy and the active participation of the faithful." Cologne and Canterbury—for all their beauty—are not the Council's models for today.

Are, then, bishops whose days are so crowded with grave administrative problems, and who have quite feasibly and unblamedly little esthetic training, to become architects and artists and men of sure taste overnight? The Council has no illusions on this point. Its instructions are clear. "When passing judgment on works of art, local ordinaries must listen to the opinion of the Diocesan Commission of Sacred Art and—in those instances which call for it—also to those of others who are specially expert" (Art. 126).

Among the "specially expert" may we not legitimately hope to find those whose lives are dedicated to art? "Bishops should have a special concern for artists, so as to imbue them with the spirit of sacred art and of the sacred liturgy." And the Council envisages the foundation of "schools or academies of sacred art . . . so that artists and craftsmen may be trained" (Art. 127). So, eight hundred years ago, did Gothic grow from all the varying French region styles when Suger called artists and craftsmen to the Ile-de-France "from all parts of the kingdom."

That it is genuinely "creative" art the Council has in mind and not a soulless St. Sulpicerie is shown in its advice to the artist. "All artists who, prompted by their talents, desire to promote God's glory in the Church, should ever bear in mind that they are engaged in a kind of holy imitation of God the Creator, and are concerned with works destined to be used in Catholic worship, to edify the faithful and to foster their piety and their religious formation" (Art. 127). *Gloriae Dei in*

Ecclesia sancta servire! Had the Fathers of the Council wished to devise a motto for the sacred art schools they envisage they could hardly have found one more succinct and more meaningful.

The future of church art, just as the future of the Church herself, depends to a great extent on the good will and the enlightenment of her priests. So "clerics are to be taught about the history and development of sacred art, and about the basic principles governing the production of its works" (Art. 129). It is the cooperation of priests so trained with the creativeness of the genuine artist that will insure the fulfillment of the Council's wishes that "all things set apart for use in divine worship should be truly worthy, becoming and beautiful, signs and symbols of the supernatural world" (Art. 122).

Discussion Questions

1. Why must a re-formed liturgy and a re-formed art go hand in hand?
2. What does Art. 128 have to say about the revision of sacred art?
3. Why is it that the Church has not adopted any particular style of art as her own?
4. What is the norm laid down for bishops in their choice of "a truly sacred art"?
5. What style of art does your parish Church contain?
6. Why should the practice of placing statues and pictures in churches demonstrate right order and a proper sense of values?
7. What does Art. 127 have to say about artists?
8. How are all artists, who desire to promote God's glory in the Church, engaged in a kind of holy imitation of God the Creator?

My Apostolate

1. The future of church art depends to a great extent on the good will and enlightenment of all her members. Consequently, I will try to learn as much as I can about the history and development of sacred art and, especially, about the principles governing the production of its works.
2. I will try to insure that the works of sacred art contained in my home are "truly worthy, becoming and beautiful, signs and symbols of the supernatural world."

The Constitution
on the Sacred Liturgy
and
Motu Proprio of Pope Paul VI

Constitution on the Sacred Liturgy

Introduction

1. This sacred Council has several aims in view: it desires to impart an ever increasing vigor to the Christian life of the faithful; to adapt more suitably to the needs of our own times those institutions which are subject to change; to foster whatever can promote union among all who believe in Christ; to strengthen whatever can help to call the whole of mankind into the household of the Church. The Council therefore sees particularly cogent reasons for undertaking the reform and promotion of the liturgy.

2. For the liturgy, "through which the work of our redemption is accomplished,"[1] most of all in

[1] Secret Prayer, ninth Sunday after Pentecost. This translation, by Father Clifford Howell, S.J. did not have the footnotes in the edition published by Messrs. Whitegate Publications. We have put in the footnotes from the original Latin version and have added some others, most of them taken from the notes to the French version published by *La Maison Dieu*. All those which are not in the original are put between brackets. There are three small emendations in the text which are not in the version published by Messrs. Whitegate Publications.

the divine sacrifice of the eucharist, is the outstanding means whereby the faithful may express in their lives, and manifest to others, the mystery of Christ and the real nature of the true Church. It is of the essence of the Church that she be both human and divine, visible and yet invisibly equipped, eager to act and yet intent on contemplation, present in this world and yet not at home in it; and she is all these things in such wise that in her the human is directed and subordinated to the divine, the visible likewise to the invisible, action to contemplation, and this present world to that city yet to come which we seek.[2] While the liturgy daily builds up those who are within into a holy temple of the Lord, into a dwelling place for God in the Spirit,[3] to the mature measure of the fullness of Christ,[4] at the same time it marvelously strengthens their power to preach Christ, and thus shows forth the Church, to those who are outside, as a sign lifted up among the nations[5] under which the scattered children of God may be gathered together[6] until there is one sheepfold and one shepherd.[7]

3. Wherefore the sacred Council judges that the following principles concerning the promotion and reform of the liturgy should be called to mind, and that practical norms should be established.

Among these principles and norms there are some which both can and should be applied to the Roman rite and also to all the other rites. The

[2] See Hebrews, 13, 14.
[3] See Eph. 2, 21-22.
[4] See Eph. 4, 13.
[5] See Isaias 11, 12.
[6] See John 11, 52.
[7] See John 10, 16.

practical norms which follow, however, should be taken as applying only to the Roman rite, except for those which, in the very nature of things, affect other rites as well.

4. Lastly, in faithful obedience to tradition, the sacred Council declares that holy Mother Church holds all lawfully acknowledged rites to be of equal right and dignity; that she wishes to preserve them in the future and to foster them in every way. The Council also desires that, where necessary, the rites be revised carefully in the light of sound tradition, and that they be given new vigor to meet the circumstances and needs of modern times.

Chapter I

General Principles for the Restoration and Promotion of the Sacred Liturgy

1. THE NATURE OF THE SACRED LITURGY AND ITS IMPORTANCE IN THE CHURCH'S LIFE

5. God who "wills that all men be saved and come to the knowledge of truth" (1 Tim. 2, 4), "who in diverse manners spoke in times past to the fathers by the prophets" (Heb. 1, 1), when the fullness of time had come, sent his Son, the Word made flesh, anointed by the Holy Spirit, to preach the gospel to the poor, to heal the contrite of heart,[8] to be a "bodily and spiritual medicine,"[9] the Mediator between God and man.[10] For his humanity, united with the person of the Word, was the in-

---

[8] See Isaias 61, 1; Luke 4, 18.

[9] See St. Ignatius of Antioch, *Ad Ephesios* 7, 2; ed. F. X. Funk, *Patres Apostolici*, Tubingen, 1901, p. 218.

[10] See 1 Tim. 2, 5.

strument of our salvation. Therefore in Christ "the perfect achievement of our reconciliation came forth, and the fullness of divine worship was given to us."[11]

The wonderful works of God among the people of the Old Testament were but a prelude to the work of Christ the Lord in redeeming mankind and giving perfect glory to God. He achieved his task principally by the paschal mystery of his blessed passion, resurrection from the dead and glorious ascension, whereby "dying, he destroyed our death and rising, he restored our life."[12] For it was from the side of Christ as he slept the sleep of death upon the Cross that there came forth "the wondrous sacrament of the whole Church."[13]

6. Just as Christ was sent by the Father, so also he sent the apostles, filled with the Holy Spirit. This he did that, by preaching the gospel to every creature,[14] they might proclaim that the Son of God, by his death and resurrection, had freed us from the power of Satan[15] and from death, and brought us into the kingdom of his Father. His purpose also was that they might accomplish the work of salvation which they had proclaimed, by means of sacrifice and sacraments, around which the entire liturgical life revolves. Thus by baptism men are

---

[11] *Sacramentarium Veronense* (Leonianum): ed. C. Mohlberg, Rome, 1956, n. 1265, p. 162; (see St. Thomas Aquinas, *Summa Theologiae*, III, 48, 6; 56, 1, etc.

[12] Preface for Easter in the Roman Missal.

[13] See the prayer after the second reading for Holy Saturday in the Roman rite, prior to the restoration of the Holy Week liturgy.

[14] See Mark 16, 15.

[15] See Acts 26, 18.

plunged into the paschal mystery of Christ; they die with him, are buried with him and rise with him[16]; they receive the spirit of adoption as sons "in which we cry: Abba, Father" (Rom. 8, 15), and thus become true adorers whom the Father seeks.[17] In like manner, as often as they eat the supper of the Lord they proclaim the death of the Lord until he comes.[18] For that reason, on the very day of Pentecost when the Church appeared before the world, "those who received the word" of Peter "were baptized." And "they continued steadfastly in the teaching of the apostles and in the communion of the breaking of bread and in prayers . . . praising God and being in favor with all the people" (Acts 2, 41-47). From that time onward the Church has never failed to come together to celebrate the paschal mystery; reading those things "which were in all the Scriptures concerning him" (Luke 24, 27), celebrating the eucharist in which "the victory and triumph of his death are again made present"[19] and at the same time giving "thanks to God for his unspeakable gift" (2 Cor. 9, 15) in Christ Jesus, in praise of his glory" (Eph. 1, 12), through the power of the Holy Spirit.

7. To accomplish so great a work, Christ is always present in his Church, especially in her liturgical actions. He is present in the sacrifice of the Mass, not only in the person of his minister, "the same now offering, through the ministry of

16 See Rom. 6, 4; Eph. 2, 6; Coloss. 3, 1; 2 Tim. 2, 11.
17 See John 4, 23.
18 See 1 Cor. 11, 26.
19 Council of Trent, Sess. XIII, Oct. 11, 1551, Decr. *De ss Eucharist.*, c. 5; (Denzinger, *Enchiridon Symbolorum*, 1644 (878). This and following references to Denzinger are to the 1963 edition; the numbers in brackets refer to the earlier editions.)

priests, who formerly offered himself on the cross,"[20] but especially under the eucharistic species. By his power he is present in the sacraments, so that when a man baptizes it is really Christ himself who baptizes.[21] He is present in his word, since it is he himself who speaks when the holy Scriptures are read in church. He is present, lastly, when the Church prays and sings, for he promised: "Where two or three are gathered together in my name, there am I in the midst of them" (Matt. 18, 20).[22]

Christ indeed always associates the Church with himself in this great work wherein God is perfectly glorified and men are sanctified. The Church is his beloved Bride who calls to her Lord, and through him offers worship to the Eternal Father.

Rightly, then, the liturgy is considered as an exercise of the priestly office of Jesus Christ. In the liturgy the sanctification of a man is signified by signs perceptible to the senses, and is effected in a way which corresponds with each of these signs; in the liturgy the whole public worship is

[20] Council of Trent, Sess. XXIII, Sept. 17, 1562, Doctr. *De ss Missae sacrificio* c. 2 (Denzinger, 1743 (940.))

[21] See St. Augustine, *In Joannis Evangelium Tractatus VI*, ch. 1, n. 7, PL 35, 1428. (See St. Thomas, *Summa Contra Gentiles*, 4, 76.)

[22] ("Therefore in the whole conduct of the liturgy the Church has her divine Founder present with her. Christ is present in the august Sacrifice of the altar, in the person of his minister and especially under the eucharistic species; he is present in the sacraments by his power which he infuses into them as instruments of sanctification; he is present, finally, in the prayer and praise that are offered to God, in accordance with his promise, 'When two or three are gathered . . .'" Pius XII, in *Christian Worship* (*Mediator Dei*). CTS, London, number 19. It will be found helpful to re-read *Mediator Dei* and *Mystici Corporis* in conjunction with this section of the Constitution.)

performed by the mystical body of Jesus Christ, that is, by the head and his members.

From this it follows that every liturgical celebration, because it is an action of Christ the priest and of his body which is the Church, is a sacred action surpassing all others; no other action of the Church can equal its efficacy by the same title and to the same degree.

8. In the earthly liturgy we take part in a foretaste of that heavenly liturgy which is celebrated in the holy city of Jerusalem toward which we journey as pilgrims, where Christ is sitting at the right hand of God, a minister of the holies and of the true tabernacle[23]; we sing a hymn to the Lord's glory with all the warriors of the heavenly army; venerating the memory of the saints, we hope for some part and fellowship with them; we eagerly await our Savior, the Lord Jesus Christ, until he, our life, shall appear and we too will appear with him in glory.[24]

9. The sacred liturgy does not exhaust the entire activity of the Church. Before men can come to the liturgy they must be called to faith and to conversion: "How then are they to call upon him in whom they have not yet believed? But how are they to believe him whom they have not heard? And how are they to hear if no one preaches? And how are men to preach unless they be sent?" (Rom. 10, 14-15).

Therefore the Church announces the good tidings of salvation to those who do not believe, so that all men may know the true God and Jesus Christ whom he has sent, and may be converted

23 See Apoc. 21, 2; Coloss. 3, 1; Heb. 8, 2.
24 See Philipp, 3, 20; Coloss. 3, 4.

from their ways, doing penance.[25] To believers also the Church must ever preach faith and penance; she must prepare them for the sacraments, teach them to observe all that Christ has commanded,[26] and invite them to all the works of charity, piety and the apostolate. For all these works make it clear that Christ's faithful, though not of this world, are to be the light of the world and to glorify the Father before men.

10. Nevertheless the liturgy is the summit toward which the activity of the Church is directed; at the same time it is the fount from which all her power flows. For the aim and object of apostolic works is that all who are made sons of God by faith and baptism should come together to praise God in the midst of his Church, to take part in the sacrifice and to eat the Lord's supper.

The liturgy in its turn moves the faithful, filled with "the paschal sacraments," to be "one in holiness"[27]; it prays that "they may hold fast in their lives to what they have grasped by their faith"[28]; the renewal in the eucharist of the covenant between God and man draws the faithful into the compelling love of Christ and sets them on fire. From the liturgy, therefore, and especially from the eucharist as from a fount, grace is poured forth upon us; and the sanctification of men in Christ and the glorification of God, to which all other activities of the Church are directed as toward their end, is achieved in the most efficacious possible way.

[25] See John 17, 3; Luke 24, 27; Acts 2, 38.
[26] See Matt. 28, 20.
[27] Postcommunion in the Paschal Vigil.
[28] Prayer for Tuesday within the Octave of Easter.

11. But in order that the liturgy may be able to produce its full effects, it is necessary that the faithful come to it with proper dispositions, that their minds should be attuned to their voices, and that they should cooperate with divine grace lest they receive it in vain.[29] Pastors of souls must therefore realize that, when the liturgy is celebrated, something more is required than the mere observation of the laws governing valid and licit celebration; it is their duty also to insure that the faithful take part fully aware of what they are doing, actively engaged in the rite, and enriched by its effects.

12. The spiritual life, however, is not by any means limited solely to participation in the liturgy. The Christian is indeed called to pray with his brethren, but he must also enter into his chamber to pray to the Father in secret[30]; yet more, according to the teaching of the apostle, he should pray without ceasing.[31] We learn from the same apostle that we must always bear about in our body the dying of Jesus, so that the life also of Jesus may be made manifest in our bodily frame.[32] This is why we ask the Lord in the sacrifice of the Mass that, "receiving the offering of the spiritual victim," he may fashion us for himself "as an eternal gift."[33]

13. Popular devotions of the Christian people are to be highly commended, provided they accord

29 2 Cor. 6, 1.
30 See Matt. 6, 6.
31 See 1 Thess. 5, 17.
32 See 2 Cor. 4, 10-11.
33 Secret, Monday within the Octave of Pentecost.

with the laws and norms of the Church, above all when they are ordered by the Holy See.[34]

Devotions proper to individual churches have a special dignity if they are undertaken by mandate of the bishops according to customs or books lawfully approved.

But these devotions should be so drawn up that they harmonize with the liturgical seasons, accord with the sacred liturgy, are in some fashion derived from it and lead the people to it, since, in fact, the liturgy by its very nature far surpasses any of them.

II. THE PROMOTION OF LITURGICAL INSTRUCTION AND ACTIVE PARTICIPATION

14. Mother Church earnestly desires that all the faithful should be led to that full, conscious and active participation in liturgical celebrations which is demanded by the very nature of the liturgy. Such participation by the Christian people as a "chosen race, a royal priesthood, a holy nation, a redeemed

[34] (The Latin phrase which Father Howell here renders as "popular devotions" is *"pia exercitia."* Certainly, "popular devotions" is more meaningful in English than is "exercises of piety," which is the rendering preferred by Canon J. B. O'Connell in his translation of the 1958 Instruction, *Sacred Music and Liturgy,* London, 1959—"The word 'devotions' has been eschewed for several reasons," Canon O'Connell notes (p. 18). The Instruction says that those sacred actions are liturgical "which, from the institution of Jesus Christ or the Church and in their name, are carried out in accordance with the liturgical books approved by the Holy See, by persons legitimately deputed, to give due worship to God, the saints, or the blessed (cf. can. 1256); other sacred actions which are performed either within or outside a church, even with a priest present or directing them, are called 'exercises of piety.'" (Canon O'Connell's translation.))

people" (1 Pet. 2, 9; cf 2, 4-5), is their right and duty by reason of their baptism.[35]

In the restoration and promotion of the sacred liturgy, this full and active participation by all the people is the aim to be considered before all else; for it is the primary and indispensable source from which the faithful are to derive the true Christian spirit; and therefore pastors of souls must zealously strive to achieve it, by means of the necessary instruction, in all their pastoral work.

Yet it would be futile to entertain any hopes of realizing this unless the pastors themselves, in the first place, become thoroughly imbued with the spirit and power of the liturgy, and undertake to give instruction about it. A prime need, therefore, is some reflection upon the liturgical instruction of the clergy. Wherefore the sacred Council has decided to enact as follows:

15. Professors who are appointed to teach liturgy in seminaries, religious houses of study and theological faculties must be properly trained for their work in institutes which specialize in this subject.[36]

16. The study of sacred liturgy is to be ranked among the compulsory and major courses in seminaries and religious houses of studies; in theological

---

35 (See *Mediator Dei, AAS*, 1947, pp. 552, 555, 559; English CTS translation (*Christian Worship*), paragraphs, 84, 92, 110.)

36 (The institutes which are of pontifical rank, and can confer degrees, are *Pontificum Institution Liturgicum*. Saint 'Anselmo, Rome, Italy, and *L'Institut Supérieur de Liturgie de Paris*. The liturgical institute at Trier, Germany, is primarily for research.)

faculties it is to rank among the main courses.[37] It is to be taught under its theological, historical, ascetical, pastoral and juridical aspects. Moreover other professors, while striving to expound the mystery of Christ and the history of salvation from the angle proper to each of their own subjects, must nevertheless do so in a way which will clearly bring out the connection between their subjects and the liturgy, as also the unity which underlies all priestly training. This consideration is specially important for professors of dogmatic, ascetical and pastoral theology and for those of holy Scripture.

17. In seminaries and houses of religious clerics shall be given a liturgical formation in their spiritual life. For this they will need proper direction, so that they may be able to understand the sacred rites and take part in them wholeheartedly; they will need personally to celebrate the liturgical rites, but also should take part in popular devotions which are imbued with the spirit of the liturgy. In addition they must learn how to observe the liturgical laws, so that life in seminaries and religious houses of study may be thoroughly influenced by the spirit of the liturgy.

18. Priests, both secular and religious, who are already working in the Lord's vineyard are to be helped by every suitable means to understand ever more fully what it is that they are doing when they perform sacred rites; they are to be aided to live

---

[37] (Up to now, the liturgy has been one of the auxiliary courses, in seminaries and houses of study, according to the ordinations of the Congregation for Seminaries and Universities, June 12, 1931 (*AAS*, 1931, p. 271). (See also the Council of Trent, session 21, ch. 2, Denzinger 1728 (931).)

the liturgical life and to share it with the faithful entrusted to their care.

19. With zeal and patience, pastors of souls must promote the liturgical instruction of their people, and also their active participation in the liturgy both internally and externally, taking into account their age and condition, their way of life and standard of religious culture. By so doing, pastors will be fulfilling one of the chief duties of a faithful dispenser of the mysteries of God; and in this matter they must lead their flock not only in word but also by example.

20. Transmissions of the sacred rites by radio and television shall be done with discretion and dignity, under the leadership and direction of a suitable person appointed for this office by the bishops. This is especially important when the service to be broadcast is the Mass.

III. THE REFORM OF THE SACRED LITURGY

21. In order that the Christian people may more certainly derive an abundance of graces from celebrating the liturgy, holy Mother Church desires to undertake with great care a general restoration of the liturgy itself. For the liturgy is made up of immutable elements divinely instituted and of elements subject to change. These not only may but ought to be changed with the passage of time if they have suffered from the intrusion of anything out of harmony with the inner nature of the liturgy or have become unsuited to it.

In this restoration, both texts and rites should be drawn up so that they express more clearly the holy things which they signify; the Christian people, so far as possible, should be enabled to understand them with ease and to take part in them fully, actively and as befits a community.

Wherefore the sacred Council establishes the following general principles:

(A) *General Principles*

22. §1. Regulation of the sacred liturgy depends solely on the authority of the Church—which means on the Apostolic See and, as laws may determine, on the bishop.

§2. In virtue of authority conceded by the law, the regulation of the liturgy within certain defined limits belongs also to various kinds of local bishops' conferences legitimately established.

§3. Therefore no other person, even if he be a priest, may add, remove or change anything in the liturgy on his own authority.

23. That sound tradition may be retained, and yet the way remain open to legitimate progress, a careful investigation is always to be made into each part of the liturgy which is to be revised. This investigation should be theological, historical and pastoral. Also the general laws governing the structure and meaning of the liturgy must be studied in conjunction with the experience derived from recent liturgical reforms and from the indults conceded to various places. Finally, there must be no innovations unless the good of the Church genuinely and certainly requires them; and care must be taken that any new forms adopted should in some way grow organically from forms already existing.

As far as possible, notable differences between the rites used in adjacent regions must be carefully avoided.

24. Sacred Scripture is of the greatest importance

in the celebration of the liturgy. For it is from holy Scripture that lessons are read and explained in the homily, and psalms are sung; the prayers, collects and liturgical songs are scriptural in their inspiration; and it is from the Scriptures that actions and signs derive their meaning. Thus to achieve the restoration, progress and adaptation of the sacred liturgy, it is essential to promote that warm and living love for Scripture to which the venerable tradition of both eastern and western rites gives testimony.

25. The liturgical books are to be revised as soon as possible; experts are to be employed on the task and bishops from various parts of the world are to be consulted.

(B) Principles drawn from the Hierarchic and Communal Nature of the Liturgy

26. Liturgical services are not private functions, but are celebrations of the Church, which is the "sacrament of unity" — namely the holy people united and ordered under their bishops.

Therefore liturgical services pertain to the whole body of the Church; they manifest it and have effects upon it; but they concern the individual members of the Church in different ways, according to their differing rank, office and activity.

27. It is to be stressed that whenever rites, according to their specific nature, make provision for communal celebration involving the presence and active participation of the people, this way of celebrating them is to be preferred, so far as possible, to a celebration that is individual and quasi-private.

This applies with especial force to the celebration of Mass and the administration of the sacraments, even though every Mass has of itself a public and social nature.[38]

28. In liturgical celebrations each person, minister or layman, who has an office to perform, should do all of, but only, those parts which pertain to his office by the nature of the rite and the principles of liturgy.

29. Servers, lectors, commentators and members of the choir also exercise a genuine liturgical function. They ought, therefore, to discharge their office with the sincere piety and decorum demanded by so exalted a ministry and rightly expected of them by God's people.

Consequently they must all be deeply imbued with the spirit of the liturgy, each in his own measure, and they must be trained to perform their functions in a correct and orderly manner.

30. To promote active participation, the people should be encouraged to take part by means of acclamations, responses, psalmody, antiphons and hymns, as well as by actions, gestures and bodily attitudes. And at the proper times all should observe a reverent silence.

31. The revision of the liturgical books must carefully attend to the provision of rubrics also for the people's parts.

32. The liturgy makes distinctions between persons according to their liturgical functions and clerical rank, and there are liturgical laws providing for due honors to be given to civil authorities. Apart from these instances, no special honors are to be paid in the liturgy to any private persons or classes of persons, whether in the ceremonies or by external display.

[38] (See Trent, session 22, ch. 6, Denzinger, 1747 (944).)

*(C) Principles based upon the Didactic and
Pastoral Nature of the Liturgy*

33. Although the sacred liturgy is above all things the worship of the Divine Majesty, it nevertheless contains much instruction for the faithful.[39] For in the liturgy God speaks to his people and Christ is still proclaiming his gospel. And the people reply to God by both song and prayer.

Moreover the prayers addressed to God by the priest who presides over the assembly in the person of Christ are said in the name of the entire holy people and of all present. And the visible signs used by the liturgy to signify invisible divine things have been chosen by Christ or his Church. Thus not only when things are read "which were written for our instruction" (Rom. 15, 4), but also when the Church prays or sings or acts, the faith of those taking part is nourished and their minds are raised to God, so that they may offer him their rational service and more abundantly receive his grace.

This leads to the conclusion that, in revision of the liturgy, the following principles should be observed:

34. The rites should be distinguished by a noble simplicity; they should be short, clear and unencumbered by any useless repetitions; they should be within the people's powers of comprehension, and normally should not require much explanation.

35. That the intimate connection between words and rites may be apparent in the liturgy:

(1) In sacred celebrations there is to be more reading from holy Scripture, and it is to be more varied and suitable.

[39] See Trent, session 22, Sept. 17, 1562, ch. 8.

(2) Because the sermon is part of the liturgical service, the best place for it is to be indicated even in the rubrics, as far as the nature of the rite will allow; the ministry of preaching is to be fulfilled with exactitude and fidelity. The sermon, moreover, should draw its content mainly from scriptural and liturgical sources, and its character should be that of a proclamation of God's wonderful works in the history of salvation or in the mystery of Christ ever made present and active within us, especially in the celebration of the liturgy.

(3) Instruction which is more explicitly liturgical should also be given in a variety of ways; if necessary, short directives to be spoken by the priest or competent minister should be provided within the rites themselves. But they should occur only at the more suitable moments,[40] and be in prescribed or similar words.

(4) Bible services should be encouraged, especially on the vigils of the more solemn feasts, on some weekdays in Advent and Lent, and on Sundays and feastdays. They are particularly to be commended in places where no priest is available; when this is so, a deacon or some other person authorized by the bishop should preside over the celebration.

36. §1. Though existing special exemptions are to remain in force, the use of the Latin language is to be preserved in the Latin rites.

§2. But since the use of the mother tongue is frequently of great advantage to the people in the Mass, the administration of sacraments and other parts of the liturgy, the limits of its employ-

---

[40] (See Trent, session 24, canon 7; session 22, ch. 8; Denzinger, 1749 (946).)

ment may be extended. This will apply in the first place to the readings and directives, and to some of the prayers and chants, according to the regulations on this matter to be laid down separately in subsequent chapters.

§3. These norms being observed, it is for the competent ecclesiastical authority mentioned in Art. 22, §2 to decide whether, and to what extent, the vernacular language is to be used; their decrees are to be approved, that is, confirmed, by the Holy See. And whenever it seems to be called for, they are to consult with bishops of neighboring territories which have the same language.

§4 Translations from the Latin text intended for use in the liturgy must be approved by the competent local authority mentioned above.

(D) Principles for Adapting the Liturgy to the Culture and Traditions of Nations

37. Even in the liturgy, the Church has no wish to impose a rigid uniformity in matters which do not implicate the faith or the good of the whole community; rather does she respect and foster the genius and talents of the various races and nations. Anything in these people's way of life which is not indissolubly bound up with superstition and error she studies with sympathy and, if possible, preserves intact. Sometimes she even admits such things into the liturgy itself, so long as they harmonize with its true and authentic spirit.

38. Provision is to be made, when revising the liturgical books, for the legitimate variations and adaptations to different groups, regions and peoples, especially in the missions, provided always that the substantial unity of the Roman rite is preserved; and this should be borne in mind when

drawing up the rites and devising rubrics for them.

39. Within the limits set by the typical editions of the liturgical books, it shall be for the competent local ecclesiastical authorities mentioned in Art. 22, §2 to specify adaptations of sacramentals, processions, liturgical language, sacred music and the arts—but according to the fundamental principles laid down in this Constitution. Above all this is to apply to the administration of the sacraments.

40. In some places and circumstances, however, an ever more radical adaptation of the liturgy is needed, and this entails even greater difficulties.

Wherefore:

(1) The competent local ecclesiastical authority mentioned in Art. 22, §2 must, in this matter, carefully and prudently consider which elements from the traditions and culture of each of these peoples might appropriately be admitted into the liturgy. Adaptations which seem useful or necessary should then be submitted to the Holy See, by whose consent they may be introduced.

(2) To ensure that adaptations may be made with all the circumspection which they demand, the Holy See will grant power to this same authority to permit and direct, over a determined period of time and among certain groups specially suited for the purpose, whatever preliminary experiments may be deemed necessary.

(3) Because liturgical laws are wont to involve special difficulties when applied to adaptations, particularly in the missions, men who are experts in these matters must be employed to formulate them.

IV. Promotion of Liturgical Life in Diocese
   and Parish

41. The bishop is to be considered as the high
priest of his flock, from whom the life in Christ
of his faithful is in some way derived and dependent.

Therefore all should hold in great esteem the
liturgical life of the diocese centered around the
bishop, especially in his cathedral church; they
must be convinced that the pre-eminent manifestation of the Church consists in the full active participation of all God's holy people in the same liturgical celebrations, especially in the same eucharist, in
a single prayer at one altar, at which there presides
the bishop surrounded by his college of priests and
ministers.[41]

42. But because it is impossible for the bishop
always and everywhere to preside over his whole
flock in his cathedral, he cannot do other than
establish lesser groupings of the faithful. Among
these the parishes, set up locally under a pastor
who takes the place of the bishop, are the most
important; for in some manner they represent the
visible Church constituted throughout the world.

And therefore the liturgical life of the parish and
its relationship to the bishop must be fostered
theoretically and practically among the faithful
and clergy; efforts also must be made to encourage
a sense of community within the parish, above all
in the communal celebration of the Sunday Mass.

[41] See St. Ignatius of Antioch, *Ad Magn.*, 7; *Ad Smyrn.*, 8;
ed. F. X. Funk, 1, pp. 236, 266, 281. (See A. G. Martimort,
L'assemblée Liturgique, in *La Maison Dieu,* 1949. pp. 151-
175; Charles Davis, *The Mass as the Assembly of Christians,* in *Studies in Pastoral Liturgy,* vol. II, pp. 138-153.)

V. THE PROMOTION OF PASTORAL - LITURGICAL
   ACTION

43. Zeal for the promotion and restoration of
the liturgy is rightly held to be a sign of the providential dispositions of God in our time, as a movement of the Holy Spirit in his Church. It is today
a distinguishing mark of the Church's life, indeed
of the whole tenor of contemporary religious
thought and action.

So that this pastoral-liturgical action may become
even more vigorous in the Church, the sacred
Council decrees:

44. Each of the competent local ecclesiastical
authorities mentioned in Art. 22, §2 is to set up a
liturgical commission to be assisted by experts in
liturgical science, sacred music, art and pastoral
practice. So far as possible the commission should
be aided by some kind of Institute for Pastoral
Liturgy consisting of persons who are eminent in
these subjects, and including laymen when appropriate. Under the guidance of the above-mention-
ed local ecclesiastical authority the commission is
to regulate pastoral liturgical action throughout
the territory, and to promote studies and necessary
experiments whenever it seems that adaptations
ought to be proposed to the Holy See.

45. For the same reason every diocese is to have
a liturgical commission under the direction of the
bishop, for promoting the liturgical apostolate.

Sometimes it may be expedient that several dioceses should form between them one single commission which will be able to promote the liturgy by
mutual consultation.

46. Besides these liturgical commissions, every
diocese, as far as possible, should have commissions for sacred music and sacred art

These three commissions must work in closest collaboration; indeed it will often be best to fuse the three of them into one single commission.

Chapter II

Of the Mystery of the Holy Eucharist

47. At the Last Supper, on the night when he was betrayed, our Savior instituted the eucharistic sacrifice of his body and blood. He did this in order to perpetuate the sacrifice of the Cross throughout the centuries until he should come again; and he wished to entrust to his beloved spouse, the Church, a memorial of his death and resurrection, a sacrament of love, a sign of unity, a bond of charity,[42] a paschal banquet in which Christ is eaten, the mind is filled with grace and a pledge of future glory is given to us.[43]

48. The Church, therefore, earnestly desires that Christ's followers, when present at this mystery of faith, should not be there as strangers or silent spectators; on the contrary, through an adequate understanding of the rites and prayers they should take part in the sacred action conscious of what they are doing, with devotion and full collaboration. They should be instructed by God's Word and be nourished at the table of the Lord's body; they should give thanks to God; by offering the immaculate victim not only through the hands of the priest, but also with him, they should learn to

---

42 See St. Augustine, *In Joannis Evangelium,* Tract 26, ch. 13, PL 35, 1613.

43 Roman Breviary, *Magnificat* antiphon, second vespers of Corpus Christi.

offer themselves; through Christ their Mediator,[44] they should be drawn day by day into ever more perfect union with God and with each other, so that finally God may be all in all.

49. For this reason the sacred Council, having in mind those Masses which are celebrated with the assistance of the faithful, especially on Sundays and feasts of obligation, has made the following decisions in order that the sacrifice of the Mass, even in the ritual forms of its celebration, may become pastorally efficacious to the fullest degree.

50. The rite of the Mass is to be revised in such a way that the intrinsic nature and purpose of its several parts, as also the connection between them, may be more clearly manifested, and that devout and active participation by the people may be more easily achieved.

For this purpose the rites are to be simplified, due care being taken to preserve their substance; elements which, with the passage of time, came to be duplicated, or were added with but little advantage, are now to be discarded; other elements which have suffered injury through accidents of history are now to be restored to the vigor which they had in the days of the holy Fathers, as may seem useful or necessary.

51. The treasurers of the Bible are to be opened up more lavishly, so that richer fare may be provided for the faithful at the table of God's word. In this way a more representative portion of the holy Scriptures will be read to the people in the course of a prescribed number of years.

52. By the means of the homily the mysteries of

---

[44] See St. Cyril of Alexandria, *Commentarium in Joannis Evangelium,* book 11, chapters 11 and 12.

the faith and the guiding principles of the Christian life are expounded, during the course of the liturgical year, from the sacred text; the homily, therefore, is to be highly esteemed as part of the liturgy itself; moreover, at those Masses which are celebrated with the assistance of the people on Sundays and holydays of obligation, it should not be omitted except for a serious reason.

53. Especially on these same days there is to be restored, after the Gospel with its homily, the "Community Prayer" or "Prayer of the Faithful." By this prayer, in which the people are to take part, intercession will be made for Holy Church, for the civil authorities, for those oppressed by various needs, for all mankind and for the salvation of the entire world.[45]

54. In those Masses which are celebrated with the people, a suitable place may be allotted to their mother tongue. This is to apply in the first place to the readings and Prayer of the Faithful, but also, as local conditions may warrant, to those items of the liturgy which pertain to the people, according to the principle laid down in Art. 36 of this Constitution.

Nevertheless steps must be taken to insure that the faithful are able to say or to sing together, also in Latin, those parts of the Ordinary of the Mass which are rightfully theirs.

If an even more extended use of the mother tongue within the Mass appears desirable in some parts of the world, the procedure laid down in Art. 40 of this Constitution is to be observed.

55. That more perfect form of participation in the Mass whereby the faithful, after the priest's

[45] See 1 Tim. 2, 1-2.

communion, receive the Lord's body from the same sacrifice, is strongly commended.

The dogmatic principles about communion of the faithful which were laid down by the Council of Trent[46] are confirmed; yet communion under both species may be granted, when the bishops think fit, not only to clerics and religious, but also to the laity, in certain cases to be determined by the Apostolic See—as, for instance, to the newly ordained in their Mass of ordination, to the newly professed in their Mass of religious profession, and to the newly baptized in the Mass which follows their baptism.

56. The two parts which, in a certain sense, go to make up the Mass—namely the liturgy of the word and the eucharistic liturgy—are so closely connected with each other that they form but one single act of worship. Accordingly this sacred Synod strongly urges pastors of souls that, when instructing the faithful, they insistently teach them to take their part in the entire Mass, especially on Sundays and holydays of obligation.

57. §1. Both in the East and in the West, concelebration, whereby the unity of the priesthood is appropriately manifested, has remained in use to this day in the Church. For this reason it has seemed good to the Council to extend permission for concelebration to the following cases:

    (i) (a) On Holy Thursday, not only at the Mass of the Holy Chrism, but also at the evening Mass;

        (b) At Masses during Councils, Bishops' Conferences and Synods;

---

46 Session 21, July 16, 1562. *Doctrina de Communione sub utraque specie et parvulorum*, ch. 1-3, (See especially canons 1-3, Denzinger, 1731 (934) 1734 (937).)

    (c) At the Mass for the Blessing of an Abbot.

  (ii) Also, with permission of the Ordinary, to whom it belongs to decide whether concelebration is opportune, and to regulate the way in which it is done:

    (a) At Conventual Mass, and at the principal Mass in churches when need of the faithful do not require that all the priests available should celebrate individually;

    (b) At Masses celebrated at any kind of priests' meetings, whether the priests be secular clergy or religious.

§2. (i) It is for the bishop, however, to regulate the discipline of concelebration in the diocese.

  (ii) But each priest shall always retain his right to celebrate Mass individually, though not at the same time in the same church as a concelebrated Mass, nor on Holy Thursday.

58. A new rite for concelebration is to be drawn up and inserted into the Pontifical and into the Roman Missal.

Chapter III

Of the Other Sacraments and the Sacramentals

59. The purpose of the sacraments is to sanctify men, to build up the body of Christ and finally to give worship to God; because they are signs they also instruct. They not only presuppose faith, but by words and objects they also nourish, strengthen

and express it; that is why they are called "sacraments of faith." They have indeed the power to impart grace, but, in addition, the very act of celebrating them effectively disposes the faithful to receive this grace fruitfully, to worship God duly and to love each other mutually.

It is therefore of the highest importance that the faithful should easily understand the sacramental signs, and should frequent with great eagerness those sacraments which were instituted to nourish the Christian life.

60. Holy Mother Church has, moreover, instituted the sacramentals. These are sacred signs which bear a resemblance to the sacraments; they signify spiritual effects which are to be obtained through the Church's intercession. By their aid men are disposed to receive the chief fruits of the sacraments, and various occasions in daily life are rendered holy.

61. Thus, for well-disposed members of the faithful, the liturgy of the sacraments and sacramentals sanctifies almost every event in their lives; they are given access to the stream of divine grace which flows from the paschal mystery of the passion, death and resurrection of Christ, the fount from which all sacraments and sacramentals draw their power. There is hardly any proper use of material things which cannot thus be directed toward the sanctification of men and the praise of God.

62. With the passage of time, however, there have crept into the rites of the sacraments and sacramentals certain features which have rendered their nature and purpose far from clear to the people of today; hence some changes have become necessary to adapt them to the needs of our own

times. For this reason the Council decrees as follows concerning their revision.

63. Because the use of the mother tongue in the administration of the sacraments and sacramentals can often be of considerable help to the people, this use is to be extended according to the following norms:

(a) The vernacular language may be used in administering the sacraments and sacramentals, according to the provisions of Art. 36.

(b) The competent ecclesiastical authorities for the different regions mentioned in Art. 22, §2 of this Constitution, should prepare without delay local rituals, also as regards the language employed, to local needs. These particular rituals, harmonized with the new edition of the Roman Ritual, are to be approved by the Holy See, and then introduced into the localities for which they have been prepared. In the Roman Ritual each one of the rites is preceded by an instruction, pastoral or rubrical in nature, or referring to the social importance of the rite. These introductions are not to be omitted from the particular rituals or collections of rites which are to be drawn up.

64. The catechumenate for adults is to be restored; it shall comprise several distinct steps, and be taken into use as and when the local ordinary may see fit. By this means the time of the catechumenate, which is intended as a period of suitable instruction, may be sanctified by sacred rites to be celebrated after successive intervals of time.

65. In mission territories it is found that some of the peoples already make use of initiation rites. Elements from these, when capable of being adapted to Christian purposes, may be admitted along with those already found in Christian tradi-

tion, according to the principles laid down in Arts.
37-40 of this Constitution.

66. Both of the rites for the baptism of adults
are to be revised; not only the simpler rite, but
also the more solemn one which must take into
account the restored catechumenate. A special
Mass "For the Conferring of Baptism" is to be
inserted into the Roman Missal.

67. The rite for the baptism of infants is also
to be revised, and it should be adapted to the circumstance that those to be baptized are, in fact,
infants. The roles of parents and godparents, and
also their duties, should be brought out more
clearly in the rite itself.

68. The baptismal rite should contain variants, to
be used at the discretion of the local ordinary, for
occasions when many are to be baptized together.
Also a shorter rite is to be drawn up for use chiefly
by catechists in mission territories, but also by the
faithful in general when there is danger of death,
yet neither priest nor deacon is available.

69. In place of the rite called *"Ordo supplendi
omissa super infantem baptizatum,"* a new rite is
to be drawn up. This should manifest more fittingly and clearly that the infant, baptized by the
short rite, has already been received into the
Church.

And a new rite also is to be drawn up for converts who have already been validly baptized; it
should indicate that they are now admitted to
communion with the Church.

70. Except during Eastertide baptismal water
may be blessed within the rite of baptism itself by
an approved shorter formula.

71. The rite of confirmation is to be revised; the
intimate connection which this sacrament has with

the whole process of Christian initiation is to be more clearly set forth; for this reason it is fitting for candidates to renew their baptismal promises just before they are confirmed.

Confirmation may be given within the Mass when convenient; when it is given outside the Mass, the rite that is used should be introduced by a formula to be drawn up for this purpose.

72. The rite and formula for the sacrament of penance are to be revised so that they more clearly express both the nature and effects of the sacrament.

73. "Extreme Unction," which may also and more fittingly be called "The Anointing of the Sick," is not a sacrament reserved only for those who are at the point of death. Hence, as soon as any one of the faithful begins to be in danger of death from sickness or old age, the most fitting time for him to receive this sacrament has, beyond all doubt, arrived.

74. In addition to separate rites for anointing and for viaticum, a continuous rite is to be prepared in which the sick man is anointed after he has made his confession and before he receives viaticum.

75. The number of the anointings is to be adapted to the occasion, and the prayers which accompany the anointings are to be revised so as to correspond with the varying conditions of the sick who receive the sacrament.

76. Both the ceremonies and texts of the ordination rites are to be revised. The address given by the bishop at the beginning of each ordination or consecration may be in the mother tongue.

When a bishop is consecrated, the laying on of hands may be done by all the bishops present.

77. The marriage rite now found in the Roman

Ritual is to be revised and enriched in such a way that the grace of the sacrament is more clearly signified and the duties of the spouses are impressed upon them.

"If any regions are wont to use other praiseworthy customs and ceremonies when celebrating the sacrament of matrimony, the sacred Synod earnestly desires that these be wholly retained."[47]

Moreover the competent ecclesiastical authority mentioned in Art. 22, §2 of this Constitution is free to devise its own rite suited to place and people, according to the provision of Art. 63. But the rite must always conform to the law that the priest assisting at the marriage must ask for and obtain the consent of the contracting parties.

78. Matrimony is normally to be celebrated within the Mass, after the reading of the Gospel and the homily, just before the Prayer of the Faithful. The Prayer for the Bride, duly amended to remind both spouses of their equal obligation to remain faithful to each other, may be said in the mother tongue.

But if matrimony is contracted apart from Mass, the Epistle and Gospel from the Nuptial Mass are to be read as an introduction to the ceremony, and the spouses should always be given a blessing.

79. The sacramentals are to undergo a revision which takes into account the basic principles for enabling the faithful to participate intelligently, actively and easily. The circumstances of our own days must also be considered. When rituals are revised, as laid down in Art. 63, it is lawful even to add new sacramentals as the need for these becomes apparent.

---

[47] Trent, Session 24, Nov. 11, 1563, De Reformatione, ch. 1. See *Rituale Romanum,* tit. VIII, c. II, n. 6.

Reserved blessings shall be very few; reservations shall be in favor only of bishops or ordinaries.

There are to be some sacramentals which, at least in special circumstances and at the discretion of the ordinary, may be administered by suitably qualified lay persons.

80. The rite for the Consecration of Virgins at present found in the Roman Pontifical is to be revised.

To promote uniformity, moderation and dignity in the ceremonies of religious profession and renewal of vows, a special rite for these occasions is to be drawn up. Apart from special exceptions granted by law, this rite should be adopted by those who make their profession or renewal of vows during Mass.

It is recommended that religious profession be made within the Mass.

81. The rite for the burial of the dead should express more clearly the paschal character of Christian death, and should correspond more closely to the circumstances and traditions found among the peoples in different part of the world. This holds good also for the liturgical colors to be used.

82. The rite for burial of infants is to be revised, and a special Mass for the occasion should be provided.

Chapter IV

Of the Divine Office

83. Christ Jesus, high priest of the new and eternal covenant, taking human nature, introduced into this earthly exile that hymn which is sung throughout all ages in the halls of heaven. He joins the entire community of mankind to himself, as-

sociating it with his own singing of this canticle of divine praise.

For he continues his priestly work through the agency of his Church which is ceaselessly engaged in praising the Lord and interceding for the salvation of the whole world. She does this, not only by celebrating the eucharist, but also in other ways, especially by praying the divine office.

84. By a tradition going back to early Christian times, the divine office is devised so that the whole course of the day and night is made holy by the praise of God. Therefore when this wonderful song of praise is duly performed by priests and others who are deputed for this purpose by the Church's ordinance, or when the faithful pray together with the priest in the approved form, then it is truly the voice of the Bride addressed to her Bridegroom; it is the very prayer which Christ himself, together with his body, offers to the Father.

85. Hence all who render this service are not only fulfilling a duty of the Church, but also are sharing in the greatest honor of Christ's spouse for by duly offering these praises to God they are standing before God's throne in the name of their Mother the Church.

86. Priests who are engaged in the pastoral ministry will offer the praises of the hours with greater fervor the more vividly they realize that they must heed St. Paul's exhortation: "Pray without ceasing" (1 Thess. 5, 17). For the work in which they labor will effect nothing and bring forth no fruit except by the power of the Lord who said: "Without me you can do nothing" (John 15, 5). That is why the apostles decided to institute deacons, for they said: "We will devote ourselves to prayer and to ministry of the word" (Acts 6, 4).

87. In order that the divine office may be better and more perfectly prayed in existing circumstances, whether by priests or by other members of the Church, the sacred Council, carrying further the restoration already so happily begun by the Apostolic See, has seen fit to decree as follows concerning the office of the Roman rite.

88. Because the purpose of the office is to sanctify the day, the traditional sequence of the hours is to be restored so that they may be genuinely related again to the time of the day when they are prayed, as far as this may be possible. To effect all this, it will be necessary to take into account the modern conditions in which daily life has to be lived, especially by those who are called to labor in apostolic works.

89. Therefore when the office is revised, these principles are to be observed:

(a) By the venerable tradition of the universal Church, Lauds as morning prayer and Vespers as evening prayer are the two hinges on which the daily office turns; hence they are to be considered as the chief hours and are to be celebrated as such.

(b) Compline is to be drawn up so that it will be a suitable prayer for the end of the day.

(c) The hour known as Matins, although it should retain the character of nocturnal praise when celebrated in choir, shall be adapted so that it may be recited at any hour of the day; it is to be made up of fewer psalms and longer readings.

(d) The hour of Prime is to be suppressed.

(e) In choir the hours of Terce, Sext and None are to be observed. But outside choir it will be lawful to select any one of these three, according to the time of the day.

90. The divine office, because it is the public prayer of the Church, is a source of piety and nourishment for personal prayer. And therefore priests and all others who take part in the divine office are earnestly exhorted in the Lord to attune their minds to their voices when praying it. The better to achieve this, let them take steps to improve their understanding of the liturgy and of the Bible, especially of the psalms.

Those who undertake the revision of the divine office are to adapt its ancient and venerable treasures so that all those to whom they are handed on may more extensively and easily draw profit from them.

91. So that it may really be possible in practice to observe the course of the hours proposed in Art. 89, the psalms are no longer to be distributed throughout one week, but through some longer period of time.

The work of revising the psalter, already happily begun, is to be finished as soon as possible, and is to take into account the style of Christian Latin, the liturgical use of psalms also when they are to be sung, and the entire tradition of the Latin Church.

92. As regards the readings, the following points are to be observed:

(a) Readings from sacred Scripture should be arranged so that the riches of God's word may be easily accessible in more abundant measure;

(b) Readings excerpted from the works of the fathers, doctors and other ecclesiastical writers should form a better selection;

(c) The accounts of martyrdom or lives of the saints are to accord with the facts of history.

93. To whatever extent may seem desirable, the

hymns are to be restored to their original form, being purged of whatever smacks of mythology or ill accords with Christian piety. Also, as occasion may arise, let other selections from the treasury of hymns be incorporated into the divine office.

94. That the day may be truly sanctified, and that the hours themselves may be recited with spiritual advantage, it is best that each of them be prayed at a time which more or less corresponds with its true canonical time.

95. Communities obliged to choral office are bound to celebrate the office in choir every day in addition to their conventual Mass. In particular:

(a) Orders of Canons Regular, monks and nuns and of other regulars bound by law or constitutions to choral office must celebrate the entire office.

(b) Cathedral or collegiate chapters are bound to recite those parts of the office imposed on them by general or particular law.

(c) All members of the above communities who are in major orders or who are solemnly professed, except for the laybrothers, are bound to recite privately whichever canonical hours they do not sing in choir.

96. Clerics not bound to office in choir, if they are in major orders, are bound to pray the entire office every day, either in common or privately, as laid down in Art. 89.

97. The occasions on which parts of the office may be replaced by liturgical services are to be defined by the rubrics.

In particular cases, and for adequate reasons, ordinaries can dispense their subjects wholly or in part from the obligation of reciting the divine office, or they may commute the obligation.

98. Religious who, according to their constitu-

tions, are to recite parts of the divine office, are thereby joining in the public prayer of the Church.

The same may be said of those who, in virtue of their constitution, recite any short office provided this be drawn up after the pattern of the divine office and has been duly approved.

99. Since the divine office is the voice of the Church, that is, of the whole mystical body publicly praising God, those clerics who are not obliged to office in choir, especially priests who live together, or assemble for any purpose, are urged to pray at least some part of the divine office in common.

All who pray the divine office, whether in choir or in common, should fulfill the task entrusted to them as perfectly as possible; this refers not only to the internal devotion of their minds but also to their external deportment.

It is strongly recommended, also, that the office, both in choir and in common, should be sung when possible.

100. Parish priests should see to it that the chief hours, especially Vespers, are celebrated in common in the church on Sundays and the more solemn feasts. And the laity, too, are encouraged to pray the divine office, either with the priests, or among themselves, or even individually.

101. §1. According to the ancient tradition of the Latin rite, clerics must use the Latin language in the divine office. But in individual cases the ordinary has power to grant the use of the vernacular to those clerics for whom Latin constitutes a grave obstacle to their praying the office as it should be prayed. The vernacular version, however, must be one that is drawn up according to the provisions of Art. 36.

§2. The competent superior has power to concede the use of the vernacular for the divine office, even in choir, to religious, including men who are not clerics. The version, however, must be one that is approved.

§3. Any cleric bound to divine office fulfills his obligation if he prays the office in the vernacular together with a gathering of the faithful or with those detailed in §2 above, provided that the text used is one that is approved.

Chapter V

Of the Liturgical Year

102. Holy Mother Church considers it her duty to celebrate the saving work of her divine Spouse by devoutly recalling it to mind on certain days throughout the course of the year. Every week, on the day which she has called "The Lord's Day," she keeps the memory of her Lord's resurrection; once in the year, by the most solemn festival of the Pasch, she celebrates his resurrection together with his blessed passion.

As each year passes by, she unfolds the whole mystery of Christ, from the incarnation and birth until the ascension, the day of Pentecost and the expectation of blessed hope and of the coming of the Lord.

Reflecting thus upon the mysteries of redemption, the Church opens to the faithful the riches of her Lord's powers and merits, so that these are in some way made present for all time, and the faithful are enabled to lay hold upon them and become filled with saving grace.

103. In celebrating this annual cycle of Christ's mysteries, Holy Church honors with special love

the Blessed Mary, Mother of God, who is insepara-
bly involved in the saving work of her Son. In her
the Church holds up and admires the most perfect
fruit of the redemption, and joyfully contemplates,
as in a faultless image, that which she herself desires
and hopes wholly to be.

104. The Church has also included in the annual
cycle days devoted to the memory of her martyrs
and her other saints. Raised up to perfection by the
manifold grace of God, and already in possession
of eternal salvation, they sing God's perfect praise
in heaven and offer prayers for us. By celebrating
the passage of these saints from earth to heaven
the Church proclaims the paschal mystery achieved
in those who have suffered and been glorified with
Christ; she proposes them to the faithful as examples drawing all to the Father through Christ, and
through their merits she pleads for God's favors.

105. Finally, at various times of the year and
according to traditional methods of training, the
Church completes the formation of the faithful by
means of pious practices for soul and body, by
instruction, prayer and works of penance and of
mercy.

Accordingly the sacred Council has seen fit to
decree as follows:

106. By a tradition handed down from the
apostles and going back to the very day of Christ's
resurrection, the Church celebrates the paschal
mystery every eighth day; with good reason this,
then, bears the name of "the Lord's Day" or "Sunday." For on this day Christ's faithful should come
together into one place so that, by hearing the
word of God and taking part in the eucharist, they
may call to mind the passion, resurrection and
glorification of the Lord Jesus, and may thank God

who "has begotten them again, through the resurrection of Jesus Christ from the dead, unto a living hope" (1 Pet. 1, 3). Hence the Lord's Day is the original feastday to be proposed to the piety of the faithful, and they should be taught to observe it as a day of joy and of freedom from work. Other celebrations, unless they be truly of great importance, must not have precedence over the Sunday which is the foundation and kernel of the whole liturgical year.

107. The liturgical year is to be revised so that the traditional customs and training methods of the sacred seasons shall be preserved, or else restored to suit the conditions of modern times; their specific character is to be retained, so that they duly nourish the piety of the faithful who celebrate the mysteries of Christian redemption, especially the paschal mystery. If certain adaptations are considered necessary on account of local conditions, they are to be made in accordance with the provisions of Arts. 39 and 40.

108. The minds of the faithful must be directed primarily toward the feasts of the Lord whereby the mysteries of salvation are celebrated in the course of the year. Therefore the proper of the time must be given the preference which is its due over the feasts of the saints, so that the entire cycle of the mysteries of salvation may be suitably recalled.

109. The season of Lent has a twofold character; primarily by recalling or preparing for baptism and penance, it disposes the faithful who persevere in hearing the word of God and in prayer, to celebrate the paschal mystery. This twofold character is to be brought into greater prominence both in the liturgy and by instruction. Hence:

(a) More use is to be made of the baptismal features proper to the lenten liturgy; some of them, which used to flourish in bygone days, are to be restored as may seem good.

(b) The same is to apply to the penitential elements. As regards instruction it is important to impress on the minds of the faithful not only the social consequences of sin but also that essence of the virtue of penance which leads to the detestation of sin as an offense against God; the role of the Church in penitential practices is not to be passed over, and the people must be exhorted to pray for sinners.

110. During Lent penance should not be only internal and individual, but also external and social. The practice of penance should be fostered in ways that are possible in our own times and in different regions, and according to the circumstances of the faithful; it should be warmly encouraged by the authorities mentioned in Art. 22.

Let the sacred paschal fast be observed everywhere on Good Friday and, where possible, let it be prolonged throughout Holy Saturday, so that the joys of Easter Sunday may be attained with uplifted and clear minds.

111. The saints have been traditionally honored in the Church and their authentic relics and images are held in veneration. For the feasts of the saints proclaim the wonderful works of Christ in his servants, and display to the faithful fitting examples for their imitation.

Lest the feasts of the saints should take precedence over the feasts which commemorate the very mysteries of salvation, many of them should be left to be celebrated by some particular church or nation or religious order; only those should be extended to the universal Church which commemorate saints who are truly of universal importance.

Appendix

A Declaration
of the Second Vatican Council
on Revision of the Calendar

The Second Ecumenical Sacred Council of the Vatican, recognizing the importance of the wishes expressed by many concerning a fixed Easter and an unchanging calendar, having carefully considered the effects which could result from the introduction of a new calendar, declares as follows:

1. The sacred Council would not object if the feast of Easter were assigned to a particular Sunday of the Gregorian Calendar, provided that others whom it may concern, especially the brethren who are not in communion with the Holy See, are agreed on this matter.

2. The sacred Council likewise declares that it does not oppose efforts designed to introduce a perpetual calendar into civil society.

But, among the various systems which are being suggested to stabilize a perpetual calendar and to introduce it into civil life, only some will be unopposed by the Church. These are the systems which retain and safeguard a seven-day week with Sunday, and which do not insert any extra days considered as belonging to no week, so that the succession of weeks may be left intact as far as possible. If serious reasons appear to dictate otherwise, the Holy See will judge of them.

Chapter VI

Of Sacred Music

112. The musical tradition of the universal Church is a treasure of inestimable value, greater even than that of any other art. The main reason for this pre-eminence is that, as sacred song united to the words, it forms a necessary or integral part of the solemn liturgy.

Holy Scripture, indeed, has bestowed praise upon sacred song, and the same may be said of the Fathers of the Church and of the Roman pontiffs who in recent times, led by St. Pius X, have explained more precisely the ministerial function supplied by sacred music in the service of the Lord.

Therefore sacred music is to be considered the more holy in proportion as it is more closely connected with the liturgical action, whether it adds delight to prayer, fosters unity of minds, or confers greater solemnity upon the sacred rites. For the Church approves of all forms of true art having the needed qualities, and admits them into divine worship.

Accordingly the sacred Council, keeping to the norms and precepts of ecclesiastical tradition and discipline, and having regard to the purpose of sacred music—which is the glory of God and the sanctification of the faithful—decrees as follows:

113. Liturgical worship is given a more noble form when the divine offices are celebrated solemnly in song, with the assistance of sacred ministers and the active participation of the people.

As regards the language to be used, the provisions of Art. 36 are to be observed; for the Mass,

Art. 54; for the sacraments, Art. 63; for the divine office, Art. 101.

114. The treasury of sacred music is to be preserved and fostered with great care. Choirs must be diligently promoted, especially in cathedrals; bishops and other pastors of souls must be at pains to insure that, whenever the sacred liturgy is to be solemnized with song, the whole body of the faithful may be able to contribute that active participation which is rightly theirs, as laid down in Arts. 28 and 30.

115. Great importance is to be attached to the teaching and practice of music in seminaries, in the novitiates and houses of study of religious of both sexes, and also in other Catholic schools and institutions. To impart this instruction, teachers are to be carefully trained and put in charge of the teaching of sacred music.

It is desirable also to found higher institutes of sacred music whenever this can be done.

Composers and singers, especially boys, must be given also a genuine liturgical training.

116. The Church acknowledges Gregorian Chant as specially suited to the Roman liturgy; therefore, other things being equal, it should be given pride of place in liturgical functions.

But other kinds of sacred music, especially polyphony, are by no means excluded from liturgical celebrations, so long as they accord with the spirit of the liturgical action, as laid down in Art. 30.

117. The typical editions of the liturgical songbooks are to be completed; and a more critical edition is to be prepared of those books already published since the restoration of sacred music by St. Pius X.

It is desirable also that an edition be brought

out containing simpler chants, for use in small churches.

118. Religious singing by the people is to be skillfully fostered, so that in popular devotions, as also during liturgical services, the voices of the faithful may ring out according to the norms and requirements of the rubrics.

119. In certain parts of the world, especially in the mission lands, there are nations which have their own musical traditions, and these play a great part in their religious and social life. For this reason due importance is to be attached to their music, and a suitable place is to be given to it, not only in forming their attitude toward religion, but also in adapting worship to their native genius, as indicated in Arts. 39 and 40.

Therefore when missionaries are being given training in music, every effort should be made to see that they become competent in promoting the traditional music of these peoples, both in schools and in the liturgy, as far as may be practicable.

120. In the Latin Church preference is to be given to the pipe organ, for it is the traditional musical instrument which adds a wonderful splendor to the Church's ceremonies and powerfully lifts up man's mind to God and to higher things.

But other instruments also may be admitted for use in divine worship, with the knowledge and consent of the competent territorial authorities as laid down in Arts. 22, §2, 37 and 40. This may be done, however, only on condition that the instruments are suitable, or can be made suitable, for use in divine worship, accord with the dignity of the sacred building, and truly contribute to the edification of the faithful.

121. Composers, filled with the Christian spirit,

should feel that their vocation is to cultivate sacred music and increase its store of treasures.

Let them produce compositions which have the qualities proper to genuine sacred music. And they must not confine themselves to composing works which can be sung only by large choirs, but should provide also for the needs of small choirs and for the active participation of the entire assembly of the faithful.

The word-texts intended to be sung must always be in conformity with Catholic doctrine; indeed they should be drawn chiefly from holy Scripture and from liturgical sources.

Chapter VII

Of Sacred Arts and Furnishings

122. Very rightly the fine arts are considered to rank among the noblest activities of man's genius, and this applies especially to religious art and to its highest achievement, which is sacred art. These arts, by their very nature, are oriented toward the infinite beauty of God which they attempt in some way to portray by the work of human hands; they achieve their purpose of rebounding to God's praise and glory in proportion as they are directed the more exclusively to the single aim of raising men's minds devoutly toward the Divine Majesty.

Holy Mother Church has always been the patron of the fine arts and has ever sought their valued help, with the special aim that all things set apart for use in divine worship should be truly worthy, becoming and beautiful, signs and symbols of the supernatural world. The Church has, indeed, trained artists and craftsmen to make such things. Moreover she has, with good reasons, reserved to herself the right to pass judgment upon the works of artists, deciding which of them are in accordance with faith, piety, and cherished traditional laws, and thereby fitted for sacred use.

The Church has been particularly careful to see that church furnishing should worthily and beautifully serve the dignity of worship, and has admitted changes in materials, style or ornamentation prompted by the progress of the technical arts with the passage of time.

Wherefore the Council Fathers have decided to issue the following decrees on these matters:

123. The Church has not adopted any particular style of art as her very own; she has admitted styles from every period according to the natural dispositions and circumstances of her peoples, and the needs of the various rites. Thus, in the course of the centuries, she has amassed a treasury of art which must be very carefully preserved. The art of our own days, coming from every race and region, is also to be given free scope provided that it adorns the sacred buildings and holy rites with due reverence and honor; thereby it is enabled to contribute its own voice to that wonderful chorus of praise in honor of the Catholic faith sung by great men in times gone by.

124. Ordinaries, by the encouragement and favor they show to art which is truly sacred, should strive after noble beauty rather than sumptuous display. This principle is to apply also to sacred vestments and ornaments which ought not to be unduly expensive.

Bishops should carefully and insistently remove from churches and other holy places the works, produced by some artists, which do not accord with faith, morals and Christian piety, and which offend true religious sense either by depraved forms or by lack of artistic worth, mediocrity and pretense.

And when churches are to be built, ordinaries must see to it that the design of these churches is such as to facilitate the celebration of the liturgy and the active participation of the faithful.

125. The practice of placing statues and pictures in churches so that they may be venerated by the faithful is to be maintained; but their number should be moderate and their relative positions should exemplify right order. For otherwise they might provoke astonishment among the people and foster devotions of doubtful orthodoxy.

126. When passing judgment on works of art local ordinaries must listen to the opinions of the Diocesan Commission of Sacred Art and—in those instances which call for it—also to those of others who are specially expert, and of the commissions referred to in Arts. 44, 45 and 46.

Ordinaries must be very careful to see that sacred furnishings and works of value are not dispersed or allowed to fall into other hands; for they were intended to add to the splendor of God's house.

127. Bishops should have a special concern for artists, so as to imbue them with the spirit of sacred art and of the sacred liturgy. This they may do in person, or through suitable priests who are gifted with a knowledge and love of art.

It is also very desirable that schools or academies of sacred art should be founded in those parts of the world where they would be useful, so that artists and craftsmen may be trained.

All artists who, prompted by their talents, desire to promote God's glory in the Church, should ever bear in mind that they are engaged in a kind of holy imitation of God the Creator, and are concerned with works destined to be used in Catholic worship, to edify the faithful, and to foster their piety and their religious formation.

128. Besides the revision of the liturgical books ordered in Art. 25, there is to be an early revision of the ecclesiastical laws and statutes which govern the provision of material things involved in public worship. These laws refer especially to the worthy and well planned building of churches, the shape and construction of altars, the nobility, position and safety of the eucharistic tabernacle, the dignity and fitness of the baptistery, the suitable placing of sacred images, embellishments and vestments. Any laws which seem less suited to the reformed liturgy are to be brought into harmony with it, or else abrogated; and any which are helpful are to be retained if already in force, or introduced where they are lacking.

According to the principle of Art. 22 of this Constitution, the local bishops' conferences are empowered to adapt such things to the needs and customs of their different regions; this applies especially to the materials and styles of church furnishings and of sacred vestments.

129. During their philosophical and theological studies, clerics are to be taught about the history and development of sacred art, and about the basic principles governing the production of its works. In consequence they will be able to appreciate and preserve the Church's ancient monuments, and be in a position to aid, by good advice, artists who are engaged in producing works of art.

130. It is fitting that the use of pontificals be reserved to those ecclesiastical persons who have episcopal rank or some particular jurisdiction.

Motu Proprio
of Pope Paul VI [1]

THERE is abundant evidence of the constant solicitude of Our predecessors and Ourselves, and of the bishops of the Church, for the preservation, the embellishment and—where needful—the reform of the sacred liturgy. Many, and well-known, published documents testify to it. A more recent indication is the Constitution on the Sacred Liturgy, which was approved, almost unanimously, by the Second Ecumenical Council of the Vatican, and which We had promulgated in solemn session on December 4, 1963.

The reason for such solicitude is that: "in the earthly liturgy we take part in a foretaste of that heavenly liturgy which is celebrated in the holy city of Jerusalem, toward which we journey as pilgrims, where Christ is sitting at the right hand of God, a minister of the holies and of the true tabernacle; we sing a hymn to the Lord's glory with all the warriors of the heavenly army; venerating the memory of the saints, we hope for some part and fellowship with them; we eagerly await our Savior, the Lord Jesus Christ, until he, our life, shall appear and we too will appear with him in glory" (Constitution on the Sacred Liturgy, Art. 8).

And so it is that the faithful, when they thus worship God, the source and model of all holiness, are themselves drawn and, as it were, impelled to holiness; though still earth-bound pilgrims, they become "contenders for the heavenly Sion, *almae Sionis aemuli*" (Lauds hymn, feast of the Dedication of a Church).

In the light of all this, it is easy to see why We so much want to see all Christians, and especially all priests, study the Constitution on the Sacred Liturgy and be prepared to put it wholeheartedly and loyally into execution as soon as it comes into force. In the nature of the case, there is need for the immediate implementation of the prescription bearing on the knowledge and the promulgation of the liturgical laws. For this reason We appeal insistently to bishops of dioceses to set at once about teaching their people the power and the interior worth of the sacred liturgy, taking into account their age, condition in life and standard of religious culture, and using the help of their priests, "the dispensers of the mysteries of Christ" (1 Cor. 4:1). Their shared knowledge will enable the faithful to take part in the religious services together, devoutly and with body and soul (Cf. Constitution, Art. 19).

It is obvious, at the same time, that several prescriptions of the Constitution need time for their implementation: certain rites have to be revised and new editions of the liturgical books prepared. To insure that this work will be carried out with the requisite wisdom and prudence, We have set up a special commission whose principal task it will be to see to the proper execution of the Constitution.

However, there are certain prescriptions of the Constitution which can be implemented at once. It is Our wish that these come into force without delay, so that the faithful will not be longer deprived of the spiritual benefits which are expected from them.

Therefore, with Our apostolic authority, and by means of this *Motu Proprio,* We order and decree that, from the coming first Sunday of Lent, which this year falls on February 16, when the *vacatio legis* shall have been terminated, the following prescriptions shall come into force:

1. It is Our wish that seminaries, houses of study of religious orders, and faculties of theology begin at once about incorporating into their curricula the prescriptions of Articles 15, 16 and 17 on the teaching of the liturgy, in such wise that they will be able to carry them out properly and diligently from the commencement of the next scholastic year.[2]

2. We decree, also, that, in accordance with the prescriptions of Articles 45 and 46, a commission be set up in every diocese whose task it will be, under the direction of the bishop, to promote the liturgy and understanding of the liturgy.

It would be advisable, also, that in some cases several dioceses should have a common commission.

Further, as far as possible, in every diocese two other commissions should be set up, one for sacred music and one for sacred art.

It will, in many cases, be convenient to unify those three diocesan commissions.

3. Further, it is Our wish that on the same date the prescription contained in Article 52—that there should be a homily during Mass on Sundays and holydays—should come into force.[3]

4. We also ordain that the portion of Article 71 which permits the conferring of the sacrament of confirmation during Mass, when opportunity offers, should become effective at once.[4]

5. With regard to Article 78: the sacrament of matrimony is normally to be administered during Mass, after the gospel and homily.[5]

We ordain that, whenever matrimony has to be

administered outside of Mass, the following prescriptions are to be observed, until this rite will have been completely revised: after a brief address (see Constitution, Article 35, §3) the epistle and gospel from the nuptial Mass are to be read in the vernacular; then the nuptial blessing, which is contained in the Roman Ritual, tit. 8, ch. 3, is on every occasion (*semper*) to be imparted.[6]

6. Although the divine office has not yet been revised and reformed in accordance with the prescriptions of Article 89, We grant to all those who are not obliged to the choral recitation of the office permission to omit the hour of Prime as from February 16, and to choose among the remaining small hours the one that is most suitable to the time of day.

In making this concession, We are fully confident that the sacred ministers will lose none of their piety as a result, rather, by performing their priestly duties diligently for the love of God, they will find themselves more intimately united to him all day long[7]

7. Still with regard to the divine office, We ordain that the faculty can now be made use of by which ordinaries in individual cases and for a reasonable cause (*in casibus particularibus et de justa causa*) can dispense their subjects from the whole or from part of the obligation of reciting the divine office, or can exchange it for another obligation (Cf. Constitution, Art. 97).[8]

8. Still further with regard to the divine office, We wish to state that when members of the institutes of perfection recite, in obedience to their rules, some portion of the divine office, or some "small office" based on the plan of the divine office and duly approved, they are to be considered as praying publicly with the Church (Cf. Constitution, Art. 98) .

9. According to Article 101 of the Constitution,

those who are obliged to the recitation of the divine office can be granted permission, in varying circumstances, to use a vernacular rendering instead of the Latin. We deem it opportune to specify that such vernacular renderings must be prepared and approved by the competent territorial ecclesiastical authority, in keeping with Article 36, §3 and 4, and that the "acts" of this authority must be approved—that is to say, confirmed—by the Holy See, in keeping with Article 36, §3.[9] And we prescribe that this is always to be observed whenever a Latin liturgical text is translated into the vernacular by the aforesaid authority.[10]

10. According to Article 22, §2, the care of the liturgy is, within certain limits, vested in territorial episcopal conferences of various types. We lay down that the word "territorial" is, for the time being, to be taken to mean "national."

As well as residential bishops, all those who are mentioned in Canon 292 of the Code of Canon Law can take part in these national conferences, with the right to vote. Further, coadjutor and auxiliary bishops can also be called to these conferences.

In these assemblies, a two-thirds majority by secret ballot is required for the making of legitimate decrees.

11. Lastly, We would draw attention to the fact that, apart from the innovations We have introduced by this apostolic letter, and apart from other changes whose implementation We have anticipated, the regulation of the sacred liturgy is vested exclusively in the Church: that is to say, in this apostolic See and, in the measure allowed by the law, in the bishop. For this reason, nobody else, not even a priest, is entitled to add, subtract or change anything in the liturgy (Cf. Constitution, Art. 22, §1 and 3).

We ordain that all that We have laid down in this

Motu Proprio is to stand firm and is to be observed, no matter what else may stand contrary to it.

Given at Rome, in St. Peter's, January 25, 1964, the feast of the Conversion of St. Paul the Apostle, the first year of Our pontificate.[11]

POPE PAUL VI

Footnotes

1. The *Motu Proprio, Sacram Liturgiam,* was promulgated on January 25, 1964. A Latin text was published in *L'Osservatore Romano* on January 29, 1964; and an Italian translation on January 31. At the beginning of March the Vatican Polyglot Press published another Latin text— "other" in the sense that there are a few, but important, differences between it and the earlier one. This second Latin text is, presumably, the official version. The translation which follows has been made from it. We have added footnotes containing lengthy excerpts from the authoritative commentary on the *Motu Proprio* by Father A. Bugnini, secretary of the post-conciliar liturgical commission. His commentary was published in *L'Osservatore Romano* on March 2-3, 1964. The text of the *Motu Proprio* and the excerpts from Father Bugnini's commentary have been translated by Father Austin Flannery, O.P.

2. Father Bugnini comments: "Since there is question of ranking the liturgy among the 'compulsory and major courses' . . . (Const., Art. 16) and since this will entail re-arrangement of the number of hours and of years devoted to teaching . . ., it is clear that the congregation of seminaries and universities can be expected to issue directives as soon as possible so that the new arrangement can be put into execution properly (*ordinate*) and with the generous and intelligent cooperation and the goodwill (diligenter) of all those involved."

3. Father Bugnini remarks that this prescription (Art. 3) merely reinforces Article 52 of the Constitution, which is itself the echo of a centuries-old tradition; he refers to canon 1345 and number 747 of the new Code of Rubrics (1960). All this is evidence, he says, of the Church's will that "the catechesis *within the Mass* should be a firm, immovable part of the pastoral ministry. No facile excuse can

exempt the priest from the duty of addressing living words to the 'holy assembly,' expounding 'what has been read,' exhorting, enlightening and comforting, enlivening and nourishing the Christian life. At Mass the priest is the mouth-piece of God to the assembly of the faithful, he is the minister and the interpreter authorized by the Church."

4. Father Bugnini comments: "It is clear that there is question of the occasions when the number of those making their confirmation is not too great, and when pastoral reasons do not counsel otherwise."

5. Father Bugnini comments: "It would seem to be preferable that the rite should be administered by the priest who celebrates the Mass."

6. Of the "brief address," Father Bugnini says: "This has the effect of erecting a first barrier against the profane, and of preparing the approach to a sacred action." Noting that the blessing is to be given "on every occasion, *semper,*" Father Bugnini remarks that therefore it is to be given whenever matrimony is celebrated during Lent and Advent, though this does not mean, he says, that license is thereby given for the pomp and magnificence that would be out of keeping with the penitential character of these seasons. He goes on: "The permission given for the administration of confirmation during Mass, and the clearly-expressed wish that matrimony be administered during Mass, are a re-statement of the principle that the Mass is the center of worship; that it is from the altar that every grace and blessing descend on the faithful. For centuries the tradition was that it was during Mass, or in close connection with the Mass, that all the sacraments were administered, all the consecrations and the simple blessings—one thinks only of the blessing of the first-fruits at the *per quem haec omnia* of the Canon. All creatures were thus transformed and sanctified by the sacrifice of Christ.

"Students of pastoral liturgy have frequently remarked that certain sacramental rites, the most relevant and obligatory for the faithful, commence abruptly, dispensing with the necessary preparation of the spirit. But when they have been inserted into their native element, they take on greater significance."

7. Father Bugnini comments: "The omission of Prime does not follow *ipso facto* from the Constitution, which merely foresees its suppression by the reform which is to be set in train, when its psalms and, perhaps, certain subsequent prayers will have been absorbed into other parts of the

divine office. This is, therefore, a real and generous concession by the Holy Father.

"These two permissions are granted only to those who are not obliged to office in choir. In other words: all those who are obliged to the recitation of office in choir must continue to recite the whole of the divine office, just as they did up to February 16. This holds good whether they are reciting it in common, or, for just reasons, have been dispensed from reciting it in choir and fulfill their obligation on their own. The matter is clearly stated in the Constitution, 95 (c).

"Here we touch on a perennial preoccupation of the Church. She has always regarded and always will regard public prayer as a great tribute of love to her divine Spouse. The Church's active life, in fact, is nourished and strengthened by the life of prayer. Canonical and religious communities are especially consecrated—by benefice, vocation and election—to prayer. It would be a grave loss to the mystical Spouse of Christ if this generous flood of prayer and petition were to decrease. It is only for compelling reasons—such as pressing pastoral obligations—that the Church will lessen the obligation of the divine office. Indeed, at the same time she reminds the priest forcibly that his obligation of maintaining contact with God does not ease during the day."

8. Describing this provision, Father Bugnini notes that while the *letter* qualifies the noun *causa* with the adjective, *justa,* the *spirit* would indicate the moral seriousness of the matter by adding the word "exceptional" and "only for particular cases."

9. Since number nine, as it appeared in the first Latin version, occasioned considerable controversy, and since this controversy has now been set at rest by the present text, it may be useful to give the relevant portion in Latin: "Quoniam vero ex Constit. Art. 101, iis, qui divinum Officium recitare obstringuntur, aliter aliis facultas fit, pro latina, usurpandi linguam vernaculam, opportunum ducimus significare, varias huiusmodi populares interpretationes, a competente auctoritate ecclesiastica territoriali conficiendas et approbandas esse, ad norman Art. 36, § 3 et 4; acta vero huius auctoritatis, ad norman eiusdem Art. 36, § 3, ab Apostolica Seda esse rite probanda seu confirmanda." Father Bugnini's Italian rendering of this last phrase is: "devono essere approvati, vale a dire confermati, dalla Sede Apostolica".

10. Father Bugnini comments: "A question of great importance and of incalculable consequences. For four centuries, all power has been reserved to the Holy See in liturgical matters (can. 1257). The bishops' role was limited to seeing that the liturgical laws were observed and to overseeing popular devotions. The Constitution has broken down this centuries-old barrier. The Church is now in process of restoring to the competent 'territorial' authorities—the word 'territorial' is designedly elastic—many problems pertaining to the liturgy, including those of the introduction, the use and the limits to the use of the vernacular in certain rites.

"It is perfectly natural that the Holy See should be anxious that the change-over from the old discipline to the new should be effected prudently and gradually, and with such guarantees as the delicacy and the seriousness of the matter demand. For this reason the provision enshrined in Article 9 cannot fail to meet with an intelligent understanding and to be a source of satisfaction to thoughtful people. . . .

"The *Motu Proprio* accords full recognition to the competence of the various territorial authorities in the matter of vernacular renderings of liturgical texts, in keeping with § 3 and 4 of Article 36. At the same time, it refers the 'acts' of these authorities to the Holy See for confirmation. It is obvious that the word 'acts' here covers the text of the vernacular rendering, and not merely the process by which the competent authority approved it."

11. Father Bugnini comments: "At the end of his discourse at the promulgation of the Constitution, on December 4, 1963, the Holy Father warned that nobody was to meddle with 'the official prayer of the Church, introducing private reforms or special rites', or to anticipate arbitrarily the implementation of the Constitution. It seems to me that the warning is addressed especially to the clergy. Any indiscretion, intemperate zeal or impulsiveness would harm and destroy the Constitution and the liturgy itself. It would be an irreparable crime, which would compromise the serious and calm labors of everybody else. It would not be constructive, but destructive, because the liturgy, 'the Church's most noble prayer, ought to remain in harmonious concord throughout the world.' It is clear, therefore, that whatever is not laid down in the *Motu Proprio,* even if it be in the Constitution, may not be effected by private initiative."

Father Bugnini then spoke of the Pope's reference (at the

promulgation of the Constitution) to the post-conciliar commissions. He went on: "Thus, with a full sense of responsibility and with a large vision of the objectives to be attained, the liturgical Constitution is set on its journey. Its steps are cautious and prudent, but certain. They do not betray timidity or incertitude, but they reveal enlightened circumspection and a wise sense of balance, insuring that the passage from the old to the new will be negotiated without loss of continuity, without sudden contrasts . . . but by a gradual, natural evolution toward the perfect restoration of that wonderful masterpiece, the sacred liturgy."

A Short Bibliography
of Liturgical Works

Papal Directives

POPE PIUS XII. Christian Worship—Encyclical Letter *Mediator Dei* in *Foundations of Renewal* (Four Great Encyclicals). New York: Paulist Press, 1964.

THE SACRED CONGREGATION OF RITES: *Instruction on Sacred Music and Liturgy.* Issued September 3, 1958. Translated by C. Howell, S.J. For a good, practical commentary, *cf.,* J. B. O'Connell, *Sacred Music and Liturgy.* Westminster, Md.: Newman, 1959. Far more satisfying, however, from a doctrinal point of view, is the French study, *Liturgie et Musique,* by A. G. Martimort and F. Picard. Paris: Les Editions du Cerf, 1959.

THE GENERAL DECREE *Novum Rubricarum* of July 1960. Translated (with Latin text) under the title *The Rubrics of the Roman Breviary and Missal* by J. B. O'Connell. London: Burns and Oates, 1960. For a practical commentary, *cf., Handbook for the New Rubrics* by F. R. McManus. Baltimore: Helicon, 1961.

Books of Reference and Introductions

DALMAIS, I. H. *Introduction to the Liturgy.* Baltimore: Helicon, 1961.

JUNGMANN, J. A. *Public Worship.* Collegeville, Minn.: Liturgical Press, 1958.

MARTIMORT, A. G. *In Remembrance of Me.* Collegeville, Minn.: Liturgical Press, 1959.

—— (ed.). *L'Eglise en Priere.* Tournai (Belgium) : Desclee et cie, 1961.

O'SHEA, W. J. *Worship of the Church.* Westminster, Md.: Newman, 1957.

Various Studies

DALMAIS, I. H. *Eastern Liturgies.* New York: Hawthorn, 1960.

DANIELOU, JEAN. *The Bible and the Liturgy.* Notre Dame: Univ. of Notre Dame Press, 1956.

DAVIS, CHARLES. *Liturgy and Doctrine.* New York: Sheed and Ward, 1961.

DIEKMANN, GODFREY. *Come Let Us Worship.* Baltimore: Helicon, 1961.

FLICOTEAUX, DOM EMMANUEL. *Our Lady in the Liturgy.* Baltimore: Helicon, 1959.

HAMMOND, PETER. *Liturgy and Architecture.* New York: Columbia Univ. Press, 1961.

JUNGMANN, JOSEF A. *The Early Liturgy to the Time of Gregory the Great.* Notre Dame: Univ. of Notre Dame Press, 1959.

——. *Pastoral Liturgy.* New York: Herder and Herder, 1960.

ROUSSEAU, O. *The Progress of the Liturgy.* Westminster, Md.: Newman, 1951.

SALMON, DOM PIERRE. *The Breviary through the Ages.* Collegeville, Minn.: Liturgical Press, 1962.

SLOYAN, GERARD S. *Liturgy in Focus.* New York: Paulist Press, 1964.

The Mass

BARDEN, WILLIAM. *What Happens at Mass.* New York: Alba, 1953.

GUARDINI, ROMANO. *Meditations before Mass.* Westminster, Md.: Newman, 1955.

JUNGMANN, JOSEF A. *Mass of the Roman Rite* (rev.
and abridged in 1 vol.). New York: Benziger,
1959.

————. *Eucharistic Prayer*. Notre Dame: Fides, 1958.

REINHOLD, H. A. *Bringing the Mass to the People*.
Baltimore: Helicon, 1960.

The Liturgical Year

DENIS-BOULET, NOELE. *The Christian Calendar*.
New York: Hawthorn Books, 1960.

FLICOTEAUX, DOM EMMANUEL. *The Splendor of
Pentecost*. Baltimore: Helicon, 1961.

JUNGMANN, JOSEF A. *The Meaning of Sunday*. Notre
Dame: Fides, 1961.

LEMARIE, J. *La Manifestation du Seigneur*. Paris:
Editions du Cerf, 1957.

PARSCH, PIUS. *Seasons of Grace*. New York: Herder
and Herder, 1963.

PREMM, MATTHIAS. *The Year Made Holy*. Milwau-
kee: Bruce, 1961.

Periodicals

The Bible Today. Published by the Liturgical Press,
St. John's Abbey, Collegeville, Minn.

La Maison-Dieu. (Organ of the Centre de Pastorale
Liturgique). Published quarterly by Editions du
Cerf, 29 Boulevard Latour-Maubourg, Paris 7e.

Liturgical Arts. Published by the Liturgical Arts Society, 7 East 42nd Street, New York, N.Y. 10017.

Worship. Published by the Liturgical Press, St.
John's Abbey, Collegeville, Minn.